A History
ROTHERHAM

ANTHONY P. MUNFORD

SUTTON PUBLISHING

C000157618

Sutton Publishing Limited
Phoenix Mill · Thrupp · Stroud
Gloucestershire · GL5 2BU

First published 2000

Title page picture: An early 19th-century engraving of the bridge seen from downstream, showing the original medieval arches either side of the Bridge Chapel. Note how the upstream end of the Chapel is cut away to fit the structure of the bridge.

British Library Cataloguing in Publication Data
A catalogue record for this book is available from the British Library.

ISBN 0-7509-2336-9

Typeset in 10.5/13.5 Photina.
Typesetting and origination by
Sutton Publishing Limited.
Printed and bound in England by
J.H. Haynes & Co. Ltd, Sparkford.

ACKNOWLEDGEMENTS

The material in this book has been compiled largely from source material held by the Archives & Local Studies Section of Rotherham Central Library and at Sheffield Archives. Thanks are due to the staff of both repositories for their help and assistance.

The illustrations are drawn mainly from the Illustrations Collection of the Archives and Local Studies Section, Rotherham Central Library. Other illustrations are from photographs taken by the author.

An early advertisement for the Hippodrome on Henry Street. (*Rotherham Central Library*)

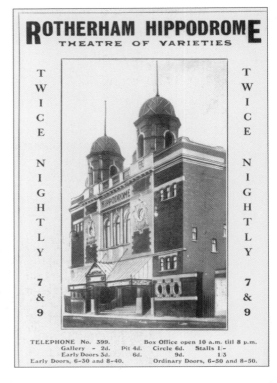

The doorway from the College, before it was removed to Boston Park in 1876. The corner of the 19th-century Court House can be seen at the right. (*Rotherham Central Library*)

Contents

The widening of Bridgegate in 1928, with newly erected shops at the right. In the centre demolition work had just started on the timber-framed Turf Tavern. (*Rotherham Central Library*)

Foreword

Inhabitants of Rotherham have a habit of claiming that 'Rotherham was a town when Sheffield was a village'. An examination of the history of the town would tend to support this assertion, at least up until the late Middle Ages. Since then no one could claim that Rotherham has not been outstripped by its western neighbour, as least as far as size is concerned. However much the national media may try to treat Rotherham as a suburb of Sheffield, the inhabitants of Rotherham know that they have a town with a history to equal its larger neighbour and most other towns in the country. With its Roman fort, parish Church, Chapel on the Bridge, College of Jesus and its rich industrial history, Rotherham has a heritage as proud as any other.

Given this history, it is perhaps surprising that no one has attempted a comprehensive history of the town since John Guest published his *Historic notices of Rotherham* in 1879. Every Rotherham historian since Guest has been deeply in his debt for he was able to examine and record many sources that have since been lost. This book is in no way an attempt to replace Guest's work in size or scope. The end of the millennium, however, seemed an appropriate time to bring the story up to date and to document at least some of Rotherham's heritage over the past 2,000 years.

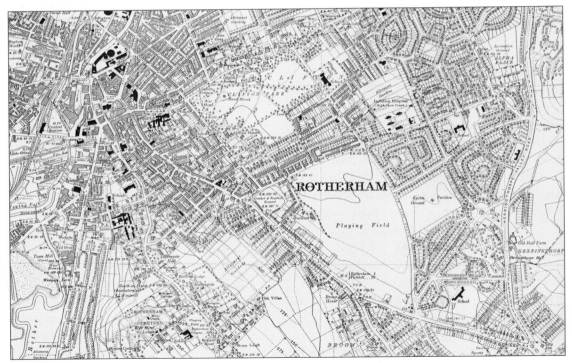

Rotherham in 1948 (Ordnance Survey sheet 289SE), showing the spread of Council housing down the west side of Herringthorpe Valley Road and the start of building at East Herringthorpe.

1

Early Beginnings

The town of Rotherham lies at the northern end of a ridge of Red Sandstone, extending south from Whiston to reach the river Don at the site of Chantry Bridge. On its western side this ridge overlooks the valley of the river Rother and its confluence with the Don a short distance to the west of the town.

It is unfortunate that there has been little systematic archaeology in and around Rotherham and our knowledge of the area in prehistoric times is based largely on chance finds. The sandstone ridge would have attracted settlement as it provided a dry site within reach of water and an excellent vantage point to spot game in the marshy river valleys below. Mesolithic flint implements, found in the 1940s in Canklow Woods and in the fields now occupied by the Duke of Norfolk Estate, and a stone hammer head from Templeborough, show that the area was settled in the Stone Age. The routeway from the south that follows the sandstone ridge down to the ford that preceded Rotherham Bridge is of great antiquity and may have already existed in the Neolithic period. The Bronze Age is evidenced by an axe found at Brinsworth and a boat of *c.* 1500 BC discovered in Chapel Dyke Flat during extensions to the steel works at Templeborough. Slightly further afield, the British Museum has a hoard of bronze implements found at Kilnhurst, *c.* 1918.

More evidence survives from the Iron Age. The clearance of Canklow Woods during the Second World War revealed a complex of banks and ditches on the crest of the valley. Amateur archaeologist Harold Copley, in 1947, was the first to suggest that these were the remains of an Iron Age settlement. Recent re-evaluation by the South Yorkshire Archaeology Service has revealed that the site is more complex than was previously realised, comprising homesteads and enclosures dating from the Bronze Age to the Romano-British period. It is also likely that the settlement originally extended further to the east, under what are now the playing fields of Oakwood School and the Hospital grounds.

Other Iron Age remains in the Rotherham area include the hill fort at Wincobank and the enclosure, Caesar's Camp, in Scholes Coppice. Neither has been fully excavated so it is impossible to assign accurate dates. Caesar's Camp, an oval 60 yd by 80 yd, is situated some feet below the crest of the nearby ridge so its purpose may not have been entirely defensive. The fort at Wincobank was much larger, 150 yd by 103 yd, with a double rampart. Partial excavations in 1899 revealed burnt stones and charred wood in the ramparts. The Roman Ridge or Rig, a double line of banks and ditches extending along the northern slopes of the Don Valley from Wincobank towards Kilnhurst and Mexborough, has long defied explanation. The one thing that is certain is that they are not Roman but almost certainly Iron Age. The Ridge takes the form of a bank with a ditch on its southern side. A detailed survey of the two lines of banks will be found in *Transactions of the Hunter Archaeological Society*, vol. 6. There have been a number of excavations along the line of the Roman Rig but none has resulted in evidence for a definitive date. Such finds as there were, including

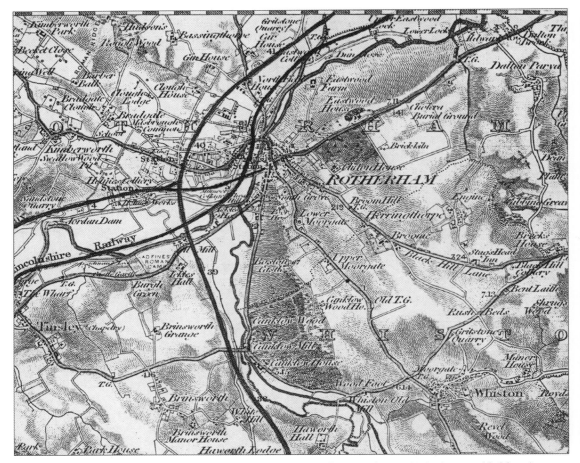

Rotherham, enlarged from the First Edition OS 1 inch to 1 mile map of *c.* 1840 (railways added later).

fragments of Roman pottery (mostly found in the fill of the ditch) and a small hoard of Roman coins found in the ditch near Blackburn in 1891, are inconclusive. Another hoard, of 3–400 coins, was found at Swinton in 1853 but the exact site is uncertain. The construction would have been a considerable work of civil engineering and presupposes an efficient, organised society. If the earthwork was defensive it must have been aimed at invaders from the south and east. Its length would have required a considerable force to man it effectively and any invading force could have outflanked it by using the Dearne Valley to the east or the Don Valley to the west. It is possible that the Rig was more of a boundary marker, delineating the southern frontier of the Brigantes.

We are on more certain ground when it comes to the Roman occupation of Britain. The Emperor Claudius invaded Britain in AD 43 and the Romans were to remain for almost 400 years. In their subjugation of the British tribes the Romans used a mixture of military conquest and diplomacy, establishing client kingdoms with pro-Roman rulers. They were able to negotiate a treaty with Cartimandua, queen of the Brigantes, a loose confederation of tribes inhabiting the Pennines. In AD 51 she proved her pro-Roman leanings by handing over the British leader, Caractacus, who had conducted a long guerrilla campaign in Wales. Brigantia was, however, far from stable as there was a considerable anti-Roman faction, led by Cartimandua's consort, Venutius. To keep an eye on the Brigantes' southern border and support their client queen, the Romans established forts at Doncaster and Templeborough in the Don Valley and at Brough in north Derbyshire.

The site at Templeborough was probably chosen because it was close to the fort at Wincobank and also to the point where Rykneild Street crossed the Don. The exact route taken by the road and the point where it crossed the river is uncertain but the Don was certainly fordable at Deadman's Hole, close to the site of the fort. The first fort, constructed *c.* AD 54, was a temporary earth and timber structure, which the legions were adept at building rapidly. It occupies a slight plateau above the marshy margins of the Don to the north and the Rother to the east. Civil war broke out in Brigantia in AD 69 and Venutius was able to seize the throne from Cartimandua. This put an end to the policy of control through client rulers and, under Agricola, the Romans absorbed northern England. Templeborough would, therefore, have ceased to be a front line fortress and may have been unoccupied for a time in the late 1st century. There is evidence that the first fort was burnt before it was rebuilt in stone *c.* AD 100. Tiles have been found on the site stamped 'CIIIIG' (i.e. the Fourth Cohort of Gauls), and it has been suggested that this unit was responsible for the original fort. More recently it has been proposed that they were responsible for the rebuilding. The cohort appears at Castlesteads on Hadrian's Wall later in the 2nd century and at Chesterholm in the 3rd century. The rebuilt fort seems to have been abandoned after the suppression of the Brigantian rebellion of AD 158. Templeborough was hastily rebuilt in the 4th century. This third fort was smaller than its predecessors and much material from the early structures, including three 2nd-century tombstones, were used in the rebuilding. The latest datable finds from the site are coins from the period AD 300–7. The earliest documentary mention of the site is not until the reign of Henry III when Ralph, son of Richard de Savile, gave a 'Templebarrow' and carucate of land at Brinsworth to Roche Abbey.

Templeborough lay at a crossroads of military roads. From the south gate a road ran to the fort at Little Chesters, Derby, and the east and west gates lay on the road that ran along the Don Valley connecting Doncaster and Brough. It is likely that the road from the north gate led, via Greasbrough and Wath, to the fort at Castleford (WRY). A civilian settlement or *vicus* grew up outside the walls to serve the garrison. Traces of this, including a possible temple site on White Hill, have been found at Brinsworth. The Romans finally abandoned Britain in 410, leaving the inhabitants to their own devices. The Rotherham area sinks into obscurity for several centuries although it is likely that the *vicus* continued to be inhabited, at least for a time after the legions left. The site of the fort remained known to future generations and it was used as a source of building stone. Some excavations of the site were undertaken in 1877 but the money ran out before much could be uncovered. It is unfortunate that in the early 20th century Templeborough lay adjacent to an expanding steel works. The demand for steel in the First World War necessitated a new melting shop at Steel, Peech and Tozer and the fort site was acquired. The borough council, realising the importance of the site, employed Thomas May to excavate the fort between November 1916 and July 1917 and much of our knowledge of Roman Templeborough depends on May's work. Since then there have been other discoveries on the fringes of the site, but the fort has remained sealed beneath the steel works.

Nothing is known about the shadowy period between the retreat of Rome and the arrival of Anglo-Saxon settlers in the Don Valley. The Humber estuary and the valley of the Don was an easy and obvious way into England for settlers from the Continent. We do not know who these settlers were but at some point a group of them decided that Rotherham would make a good site for a settlement, although they avoided the Roman remains, either through superstition or because they found a better site. We cannot say where Dark Ages Rotherham was first established but we do know that it came to be called 'Rotherham', the settlement on the river Rother, at the time. Rotherham, of course, stands not on the Rother but on the Don. Possibly the first settlement was on the banks of the Rother but was abandoned for a less marshy site, probably near the present parish church. Alternatively the place name may have been based on the Rother because there was already a town, Doncaster, which took its name from the Don. A site around the parish church would have offered a number of advantages. It lay on the old Roman road along the Don Valley and also controlled the crossing of the Don at a ford. It therefore lay at a crossroads, always a good site for a town.

No documents from the Anglo-Saxon era have survived and we know virtually nothing about life in the town at that time. Once the Anglo-Saxon settlement was complete, Rotherham found itself near the borders between Mercia and Northumbria and was almost certainly involved in the wars between the two kingdoms in the 7th century. Rotherham was probably far enough inland to escape the early Viking raids of the late 8th and early 9th centuries. Once the Vikings began to settle permanently, following the capture of York in 867, Rotherham would have found itself in the front line once again. As the Vikings pushed back the Saxon kingdoms, Rotherham found itself within the Danelaw, the area where Viking law prevailed. We have a survivor of this period in the names of several town centre streets for the 'gate' of

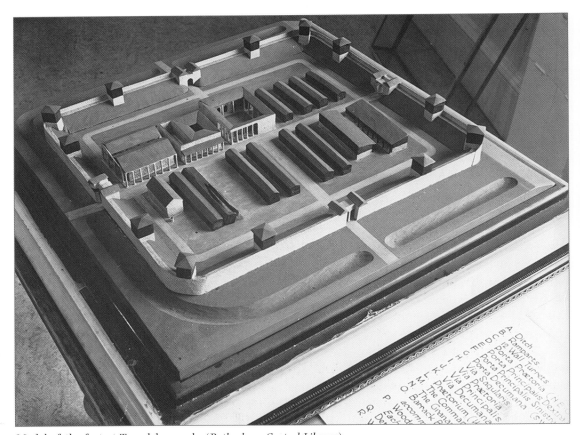

Model of the fort at Templeborough. (*Rotherham Central Library*)

Bridgegate, Wellgate, etc., derives from the Norse 'gata', 'street'. King Alfred (871–99) pushed the Vikings back to the Chester–Thames line and his successors gradually re-established Saxon power over the Anglo-Scandinavian midlands and north.

Much of the reconquest was achieved by Alfred's grandson, Athelstan (924–39). He was opposed by a coalition of the forces of Constantine II, King of Scotland, Owain of Strathclyde and the Viking, Olaf Guthfrithsson from Dublin. In 937 Athelstan's army met the Vikings and their allies at the great battle of Brunanburh and defeated them with great slaughter. Although the battle features in a number of chronicles and sagas, none of the accounts enables the site of the battle to be located with any certainty. One of the leading contenders for the site of Brunanburh is the Rother and Don valleys around Brinsworth and Templebrough. It has even been claimed that Templeborough is the 'burh' of

Column bases at Templeborough, uncovered during the excavations in 1877–8. Items of stonework uncovered in the excavations of the fort were erected at the rear of the Museum in Clifton Park. (*Rotherham Central Library*)

Brunanburh although May found no evidence for occupation of the site in Saxon times. The location is plausible as Rykneild Street would have been the obvious route for the Saxon army to take towards the Viking stronghold of York. A.C. Goodall seems to be the first to have suggested Brinsworth as the site of the battle, in his *Place names of South Yorkshire* (Cambridge, 1913). Rotherham solicitor J.H. Cockburn elaborated the argument in his *Battle of Brunanburh* (1930), and although his evidence is based on 'false etymologies and wrong-headed history' there may well be a kernel of truth in the tradition. Michael Wood (in *In search of England*, 1999) has suggested that the chapel at Tinsley may have been founded by Athelstan to say masses for those slain in the battle. Certainly in the Middle Ages the chapel was in receipt of a stipend from the Crown for saying the service for the dead, and this royal payment continued to be paid, with gaps, until the early 19th century.

In 1937 the town celebrated the 1000th anniversary of Rotherham parish church, despite the fact that there is no evidence that the church was founded in 937. The only remainder of the Saxon church is a door jamb that is now under the north-west pier of the tower. This is unlikely to be from the first church on the site, which was almost certainly built of wood. It is likely, however, that the earliest church predated the battle of Brunanburh and that the townspeople were a little late in celebrating the millennium of the parish church. The Saxon town of timber buildings would have clustered around the church, above the flood level of the river. We know nothing of the people who lived there, but we do know that in the mid-11th century the lord of the town was called Acun or Hakon, another indication of continuing Danish influence in the area. Some Rotherham men may have turned out in 1066 to follow King Harold to the victory at Stamford Bridge and the defeat at Hastings. In the aftermath of the latter battle the townsfolk found themselves with a new, alien lord, the Norman Earl of Mortain.

2

Rodreham

Early Medieval Rotherham

Rotherham emerges from the mists of the Dark Ages with the compilation of Domesday Book in 1086. This is not only the first written appearance of the name but also the first, imperfect, description of the town.

Rotherham was one of the many estates that the Conqueror bestowed on his half-brother, Robert, Count of Mortain. Both Robert and his brother Odo, later Bishop of Bayeux, accompanied William to England in 1066 and were rewarded with extensive estates. Robert was awarded a total of 793 manors. The majority of these were in Cornwall and Devon but Rotherham was only one of 196 manors he held in Yorkshire including Whiston, Treeton, Handsworth and Hooton Levitt. Robert has recently been rated by the *Sunday Times* as the third richest man in England since 1066, with a fortune valued at £46.1 billion in modern terms. He could obviously not administer all of these estates himself and Domesday tells us that Rotherham had been granted to Nigel Fossard, the earl's tenant in a number of other South Yorkshire manors, including several in the Doncaster area.

The manor of Rotherham was only one of several manors within the parish of Rotherham and comprised the township of Rotherham, on the east bank of the Don, bounded by the Don to the north, the Rother to the west, Dalton to the east and Whiston to

The Rotherham entry from Domesday Book, 1086.

the south. Rotherham's entry in Domesday Book reads: 'In RODREHAM Acun had one manor of 5 carucates taxable where 3 ploughs were possible. Nigel has in lordship there 1 plough; and 8 villagers and three bordars who have 2½ ploughs. There is a mill value 10s, a priest and a church. The whole is 10 furlongs long and 5½ furlongs wide. Value in the time of King Edward, £4 0s 0d; now 30s.'

With a church and a mill, Rotherham was already a town of some importance. Mills were not common at that period as they involved a considerable investment in construction and technology, and the Rotherham mill would have served a considerable area. Dues charged for use of the mill could bring in a considerable income to the lord of the manor.

The other information is annoyingly vague and difficult to interpret in modern terms. A carucate was the amount of land that an eight-ox team could plough in one year (c. 120 acres). There were therefore around 600 acres in the manor. Not all this was cultivable and before the Conquest there was only enough arable for three plough teams (c. 360 acres). The 72.5 per cent fall in the value of Rotherham since the time of Edward the Confessor indicates that the manor had suffered in the 'Harrowing of the North' when William I had suppressed the rebellion of 1069. There seem to have been some signs of revival in the town for Domesday Book tells us that Nigel Fossard himself had one plough team while his tenants had two and a half between them, an increase on the number of pre-1066 teams. The tenants were divided into two classes, eight villeins (unfree manorial tenants) or villagers and three bordars (smallholders). Even allowing for their families this would only give a total population of some 70 people: that seems a very small population for a town but it is likely that the entry does not allow for free tenants and tradesmen who did not work the land. The Domesday church was on the site still occupied by the present parish church. It is highly likely that the Domesday mill occupied the same site as the later town mill as good mill sites were not lightly changed.

The other manors within the parish had been awarded to Roger de Busli, lord of the liberty of Tickhill, who held 46 manors in Yorkshire and 86 in Nottinghamshire. His Rotherham manors are described as:

In CHIBEREWORDE [Kimberworth] Alsige had 6 carucates of land taxable where three ploughs are possible. Roger now there has 2 ploughs. There are 8 villeins and 12 bordars. Meadow 6 acres; woodland pasture 13 furlongs long and 1 league wide. Value before 1066 £4 0s 0d; now 30s.

In BRINESFORD [Brinsworth] Godric has 11 bovates of land taxable where 1½ ploughs are possible. Roger has it and it is waste. Value before 1066 15s.

In GERSEBROOK [Greasbrough] Godric had three carucates of land taxable where two ploughs are possible. Roger now has there one plough and three villeins and three bordars with one plough. Woodland pasture 3 furlongs long and 2 wide. Value before 1066 40s; now 20s.

Kimberworth was one of six knights fees that Roger de Busli subinfeuded (sublet) to the family of his brother Ernaldus. This line died out in the early 13th century with the death of John de Busli. Kimberworth passed to Robert de Vipont who had married John's daughter, Idonea. Upon the death of their grandson Robert de Vipont in c. 1262, the estates were divided between his two daughters, Kimberworth being assigned to the younger, Idonea, who lived until 1334 and resided at least part of the time at the hall in Kimberworth. Robert de

Vipont had a park at Kimberworth. In Edward I's *Quo warranto* enquiries of 1293–4, it was claimed that Idonea had created a deer leap around the park, to the detriment of the royal forest. The jury found that her father had indeed died in possession of a park but the deer leap (which allowed wild deer to get into the park, but not out again) was not to the detriment of the royal forest as the nearest royal forest was 15 leagues away.

Idonea married twice; firstly to Roger de Leyburn and secondly to John de Cromwell, constable of the Tower and governor of Tickhill Castle. On her death in 1334 her son John de Leyburn having predeceased her with no heirs, the bulk of Idonea's estates passed to the Clifford family as heirs to her sister Isabella. During the reign of Edward II, however, Hugh le Despenser, the king's favourite, had prevailed upon Idonea to convey portions of her estate to him, with remainder to his second son Edward le Despenser. From Edward, Kimberworth passed to his granddaughter Isabel Spencer, who married Richard Beauchamp, Earl of Warwick.

Rotherham would have been an ideal site for a castle but none was ever built there. Kimberworth still has the remains of a small motte-and-bailey castle. This may date from the early post-Conquest period or from the turbulent reign of Stephen (1135–54). It is highly unlikely that the Count of Mortain ever visited his manor of Rotherham before subinfeuding Nigel Fossard. The Fossards kept the Mortain manors in the Doncaster area in their own hands but subinfeuded Rotherham to others. In the reign of Henry I, Eustace fitz John obtained a confirmation from the king of all his lands, including those which he held of William Fossard. Eustace was killed in 1157 campaigning against the Welsh and left sons by both his wives. William, son of the first marriage, who assumed his mother's surname de Vesci, inherited Rotherham. On William's death in 1185 he was succeeded by his son, Eustace, one of the most active of the baronial opponents of King John who was killed assisting a Scots army to besiege Barnard Castle. His son, William, had two sons, John and William, with whom the de Vesci line came to an end.

The de Vesci control of Rotherham was not, however, unchallenged for the De Tilli family claimed half the manor. How they came to have a claim is unrecorded. The 17th-century Yorkshire antiquary Roger Dodsworth recorded a number of documents involving a court case between the two families. In 1200 Eustace de Vesci lodged a claim against Geoffrey de Sausensmar (or *Salicosa Mara*) and Matilda his wife, for the vill of Rotherham. In reply Geoffrey stated that his only claim to the township was in right of his wife, as her dower from her former husband William, brother of Ralph de Tilli. The case was still unresolved in 1203 and the outcome is unrecorded, but it appears to have been accepted that the de Tillis were entitled to half the manor and half the church; although from the grant to Rufford Abbey referred to below, it seems to have been accepted that the de Tillis held their half from the de Vescis.

Ralph de Tilli was also one of the barons who took up arms against King John. As a result his lands were forfeited to the Crown during the reign of Henry III, who granted Rotherham to a prominent supporter, John de Lexington, in January 1242/3. There were six Lexington brothers. Unusually the four eldest entered the Church while the fifth, John, inherited the family estate. John acted as the King's envoy to the Court of Rome in 1241, was a steward of the household in 1242–55 and Chancellor in 1247–8 and 1249–50. His brother Henry was Bishop of Lincoln (1253-58) and another brother, Stephen, was Abbot of the great Cistercian abbey of Clervaux in France. Yet another brother, Robert de Lexington (d. 1250), was the first recorded vicar of Rotherham, presented to the living jointly by William de Vesci and Geoffrey de Saucensmar in 1227.

At some point in the third quarter of the 13th century the two halves of the manor of Rotherham became united in the hands of the Abbey of Rufford (Ntt). The Lexington share was granted to Rufford Abbey in *c.* 1252. The original grant has not survived but was referred to by the abbot in 1293 when answering Edward I's *Quo warranto* (by what right) enquiry into the basis of the abbey's right to ingfangthief (the right to punish criminals caught within the manor), gallows and the assize of bread and beer with half the town's market. The de Lexington family took its name from the village of Laxton (Ntt), near Rufford, thus explaining their interest in Rufford. In return for Lexington's share of Rotherham he expected to be released from an annual rent of £30 from his manor of Averham (Ntt). In 1254 or 1255 he was also able to persuade the abbey to pay 5 marks to the chaplain serving the altar of Our Lady in the church at Laxton. This chaplain was to pray for a long list of family and friends, including Henry III and William de Vesci. When John died in 1257 his estates were inherited by his brother Henry, who only survived until 1258 when they passed to two nephews.

The abbey seems to have been intent on building up as large an estate as possible in Rotherham. As early as 1257, not long after the Lexington grant, Hugh Fraser, clerk, formerly Rector of Penistone, leased his quarter share of three mills (probably three sets of stones in one building) at Rotherham to Geoffrey, Abbot of Rufford, for the substantial annual rent of 100s, to be paid perpetually, even if the mills fell down or were swept away by a flood. He further quitclaimed (released) to the abbot his right to take timber or to pasture animals in the abbot's wood at Eastwood. Some years later (before 1283) Hugh released the abbot from paying the rent.

The de Vesci half of the manor came to Rufford some years later. The de Vescis' main estates were further north in Yorkshire where they held the castles of Knaresborough and Malton, and John de Vesci had little to lose by giving one of his remote manors to the Church in return for spiritual benefits. The original grant has not survived but the terms are known from confirmations by Edward I in 1283 and 1285. John de Vesci gave to the Abbey eight oxgangs of land in Rotherham, all his right in the manor of Rotherham with his half share in the church, the homage and service of all free tenants, the mill of Rotherham, customs, services, fisheries, mills, bakehouses, suits of mills and bakehouses, suits and profits of courts and the lordship and half the market and fair of Rotherham, all given in pure and perpetual alms (i.e. for the soul of the donor). The exact date of the original grant is unknown but it was during the term of Thomas de Stayngreve's abbacy and can be narrowed down to *c.* 1276–83. De Vesci had been a supporter of Simon de Montfort during the rebellion against Henry III and the gift to Rufford may have been a conscience-clearing act before he went on a pilgrimage to the Holy Land. It is also possible that the grant was, at least in part, a sale as the Close Roll for 1282 contains a note that the abbot owed de Vesci £93 6s.

The town's market has already been referred to. The first documentary proof of a market in the town is usually taken to be the charter of 2 January 1208 by which King John granted to Eustace de Vesci the right to have port and market at Avonmouth (Gls) and an annual fair at his manor of Rotherham for two days at the feast of St Edmund (either St Edmund the Archbishop, 16 November, or of St Edmund the King and Martyr, 20 November). Note that this charter grants a fair at Rotherham, not a market. It is highly likely (but impossible to prove) that, given its position at the crossroads of important trade routes, there would have been a market in the town much earlier.

The first definite reference to a market comes in Edward I's confirmation, dated 9 February 1283, of John de Vesci's grant to the abbey. This refers to 'the lordship of the moiety of the market and fair of Rotherham'. As there is no evidence of the grant of market rights

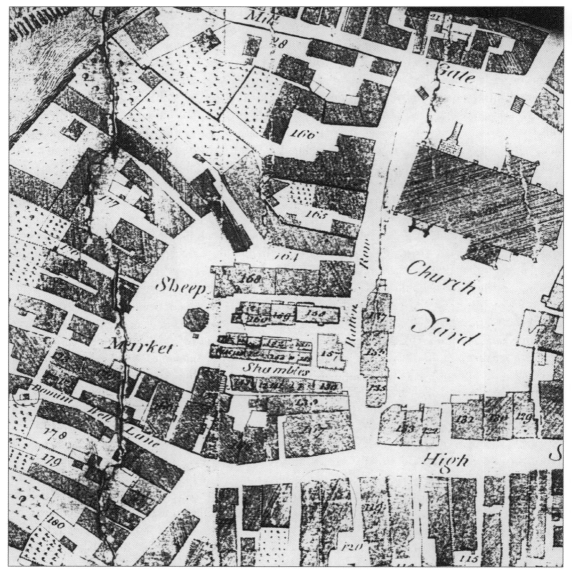

Rotherham market-place from the 1774 map of the town. Note that the only entry into the market-place was from Ratten Row via the Shambles. The building numbered 168 was the medieval Town Hall. (*Rotherham Central Library*)

between 1208 and 1283, it may be safely assumed that a market was already in existence in 1208. The abbey obtained a second confirmation of de Vesci's grant on 12 June 1285, confirming to the abbey 'all kind of judgement and correction of all trespasses as well of the evil doing of men as of assizes of bread and beer, of measures of the yard, and with the arresting and imprisoning of men malefactors found in the aforesaid lands and tenements and in the market'.

The situation becomes confused in 1307 when Edward I granted a charter to Robert de Wadsley allowing him to have a market every Friday 'at his manor of Rotherham' with an annual three day fair at the Nativity of St John the Baptist (23–5 June). To confuse the picture further, in 1309 Edward II granted to Edmund de Dacre a market every Friday at his manor of Rotherham and an annual fair for eight days at St Edmund the Archbishop and Confessor (15–22 November). The Dacre family had an earlier claim to the market. When Robert le Brun was summoned before Edward I's *Quo Warranto* enquiry of 1293–4 to prove his claim to have a fair at Rotherham with half the market and its tolls, he claimed to hold them for life by surrender of William de Dacre. To confuse matters further, this claim was for a market on Monday and a fair the eve and day of St Edmund the King (19-20 November). In turn, Dacre claimed to hold the market and fair as the inheritance of his wife Johanna. Whoever her father was, it is difficult to see how she could have had claim to a market at Rotherham unless it was some sort of residual claim from the Tillis or the Lexingtons. The fact that the claim was for only half the market would strengthen this hypothesis. There are no mentions of there being a second manor within Rotherham, and the abbot and brothers of Rufford would hardly have stood idly by and seen the grant of a market in the town in direct competition with their own. Hunter suggests that de Wadsley was farmer or lessee of the manor under Rufford. The abbey had the choice of administering Rotherham directly, appointing a steward to run the manor on their behalf, or farming it out at an annual rent. The latter course had the advantage that they would receive a fixed annual rent while the lessee gambled that he could obtain more than the rent from the income of the manor.

On 7 February 1316 Edward II granted Rufford a weekly Monday market at Rotherham with an annual eight day fair at St Edmund the King (19–27 November). This and the grant to Dacre continue the confusion between the two St Edmunds that we saw in King John's charter. If the charters are taken at face value, the Dacre fair would have overlapped with the Rufford fair.

Whatever the truth about the grant to Robert de Wadsley, he did not retain his market for long. In December 1307 he received a licence from the King to alienate lands and rents in Rotherham to Rufford, described as a messuage and toft, an acre of land, other land 46 ft by 15 ft, £9 0s 8d rent, and a rent of 1 lb pepper in Rotherham and Masbrough with the homage and service of John de Gotham, Richard Hauwys, William Malcus, William le Arewesmit, John Loselond and Hugh le Feure. This property cost the abbey 200 marks (£133 6s 8d) plus £20 paid to the king for the licence. Shortly afterwards Edmund, son and heir of Robert de Wadsley, quitclaimed to the abbot and convent of Rufford (and to one Edelma de Betecote) all his freedoms in the market at Rotherham, reserving to himself the rent from ten bakers' stalls, nine stalls for woollen cloth, six stalls for linen cloth and seven stalls to rent. It would seem from this document that certain stalls in the market had fixed uses (bakers, wool, linen) while others could be rented to any trader.

In 1320 Edmund de Dacre had a royal licence to assign to Rufford a messuage and 14s rent in Rotherham, which he held of the abbey by military service. In the same year the abbot received a grant from Sir Edmund de Dacre of half the market of Rotherham, held on a Monday, with the tolls and other profits and the fair held at St Edmund the King, together with the messuage and 14s rent. The abbey appears to have paid Dacre £95 for this grant. The money paid to Dacre and Wadsley is an indication of how keen Rufford was to gain total control of Rotherham, which was obviously seen as one of the jewels of the Rufford estate. After 1320 there were no contestants to the abbey's ownership of the manor and market. The market was obviously profitable and drew sellers and buyers from a considerable distance. Guest quotes a case of 1319 in which William Clarel, lord of Adwick le Street, accuses Robert de Raynburgh and others of obstructing a right of way at Adwick which William was wont to use 'for carrying corn and manure with horses and carts and their other necessities as well to Rotherham market as elsewhere'.

The geography of the town was to change little until the middle of the 19th century. Dominating the town centre was the parish church, ringed by the main commercial streets: High Street to the south, Brook Gate (later Jesus Gate, now College Street) to the east and Church Street (alias Ratten Row) to the west. These three streets formed the core of the town and from them radiated the roads that connected Rotherham with the outside world. Westgate ran south before turning west across the river Rother to connect Rotherham with Sheffield. Doncaster Gate ran eastwards to Doncaster and Wellgate ran south-east towards Maltby and Bawtry while another track led southwards via Whiston. Bridgegate ran from the junction of Brook Gate and Church Street, over Rotherham Bridge (or the ford which preceded it), to Masbrough and the north. The market-place occupied a sloping site on the east bank of the Don and was approached via narrow alleys from the High Street or Church Street. The cattle market was held in the Crofts at the highest point of the town. Moorgate was then a dead end, leading from the Crofts to the common grazing on Rotherham Moor. The manorial water mill was sited on the east bank of the Don reached from Church Street via Millgate. The town was surrounded by the common fields that fed it. The water supply came from the Don, from a number of public wells (such as Domine Well near the market-place) or from the springs that rose in Wellgate. The overflow from these ran down Wellgate, Brook Gate and Bridgegate, before flowing into the Don near the bridge.

The last days of Rotherham's open market-place, just before the move to the Centenary Market in 1971. The wall of the 19th-century Market Hall can be seen at the right. (*Rotherham Central Library*)

The site of the Cattle Market in the Crofts. The beast markets were held here from the Middle Ages until 1926. The site of the stalls is now occupied by the Town Hall (formerly the West Riding Court House). (*Rotherham Central Library*)

The existing weir on the river Don indicates the site of the Domesday and later corn mills. The mills stood on the site now occupied by Riverside Precinct. (*Author*)

Medieval taxation usually took the form of a grant by parliament of a levy on the value of goods or produce. In 1342 Edward III was granted a ninth of sheaves, fleeces and lambs belonging to both lay and ecclesiastical owners and a fifteenth of the goods of merchants and others not living by agriculture. A local jury of parishioners returned that the town's contribution was worth 67 marks (£44 13s 4d). The ninth of sheaves, etc. for the whole parish was valued at £29 16s. The church's annual revenues from tithes, Lenten dues and offerings was put at 10 marks (£6 13s 4d), the tithes payable by the mill came to 10s, the profits of the courts were 20s and the tithes of hay were worth £6 13s 4d. According to the jury, there were only two men whose income did not come from agriculture. Adam de Hawlay had merchandise worth 100s and the tanner Richard Tannator's merchandise was worth 10 marks (£6 13s 4d). As the jurymen were local, it is likely that they valued the town's contribution as low as they dared. Many of the tradesmen in the town would also have had lands in the open fields, and the definition of those who lived by agriculture was therefore heavily in favour of the taxpayers.

Unfortunately none of the medieval manor court rolls or the administrative records of Rufford Abbey has survived to give an insight into the running of the town and the life of its inhabitants. It is not until the later 14th century, with the introduction of the Poll Tax, that we can get any picture of the town's population structure. In 1377, the final year of Edward III's reign, the Crown changed to taxation by head or 'poll', initially levied at 4d per head on all persons over 14, with the clergy paying 1s each. Richard II, who succeeded his grandfather in June 1377, continued the tax. In 1379 it was levied on all aged 16 or over on a sliding scale according to wealth. The basic rate remained at 4d rising in stages to £4.00 for an earl and a top rate of £6 13s 4d for a duke. The clergy and the poor were exempt. The tax was introduced again in 1381, at 1s per head, but was so unpopular and led to such public hostility that, after the Peasants' Revolt, it was dropped and not tried again until the 17th century. The surviving records of the 1377 Poll Tax in the Public Record Office record only the sums raised by each township. In Rotherham the locally appointed collectors, John de Bolom, the town constable, Thomas Bakester and John de Palden delivered £5 6s to the Treasury. Kimberworth, where the constable Richard de Kymberworth collected the tax with Adam Loweson and Richard Robynson, rendered 38s.

The 1379 returns are more useful as they list everyone who paid. The West Riding returns were published in the *Yorkshire Archaeological Journal* for 1879 and show the town 30 years after the Black Death had hit Yorkshire. There is no evidence of the extent to which the plague affected the town but it is known that over half the benefices in the Diocese of York were vacated by death and 59 per cent of the clergy in the Deanery of Doncaster died. In Rotherham Rayner de Roderham replaced William Lytester as vicar of the de Tilli portion of the parish church in 1349, and it is possible that Lytester was a victim of the Black Death. It is likely that Rotherham lost a considerable portion of its population, and it had almost certainly not recovered its pre-Black Death position when the Poll Tax assessors called in 1379.

The 1379 Rotherham township returns list 356 people, men and women. This compares with a total of 528 persons for Sheffield. It is impossible to know how many clergy there were, how many children under 16, how many paupers and how many managed to avoid payment but based on the evidence of the Poll Tax the total population of the township can be estimated at *c.* 500 to 600. Including the townships of Kimberworth (89 assessed persons), Brinsworth (48), Greasbrough (108) and Dalton (61) increases the total of assessed inhabitants to 662, 25 per cent greater than Sheffield. The total population of the parish of Rotherham can be estimated at *c.* 1,000 to 1,200.

In Rotherham township there were 118 married couples and 120 unmarried children, single men and women. Women slightly outnumbered men, at 182 to 174. Including the out-townships increases the statistics to 226 married couples, 210 single men and women, 342 men and 320 women. The total value of the tax assessed on the townships in Rotherham parish was £10 16s 6d, greater than Sheffield and almost as large as Doncaster.

The assessment shows that there was no resident lord and there is no-one that can be identified as the steward for Rufford Abbey. The top of the Rotherham social pyramid was occupied by a merchant, John Mersburg' (Masbrough) and his wife Elisot, who paid 10s. At the next level down were Robert de Boln, merchant, who paid 5s; John de Palden, 'barker' (tanner) at 40d: Thomas Bakester, 'osteler', William de Mapples, 'barker', and William Baker, baker, who paid 2s. Below them was a layer of lesser tradesmen who paid 12d or 6d and 224 who paid the basic 4d. A number of households employed servants even among the lower strata of society. John de Berneslay paid only the basic 4d but had three servants.

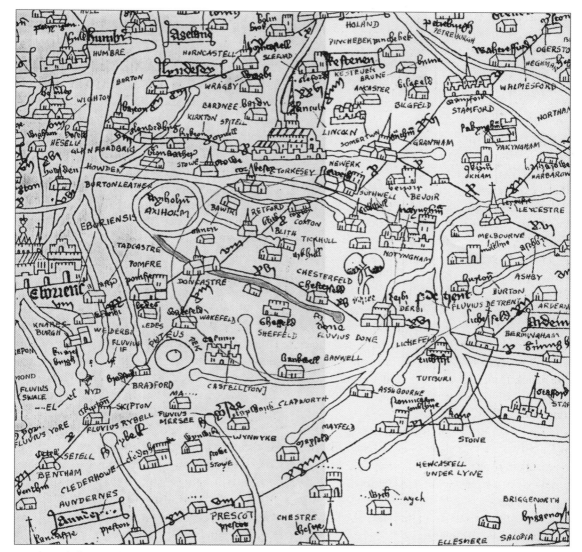

South Yorkshire in the 14th century. An extract from Gough's Map of Britain, dating from 1325–50, which marks Doncaster and Sheffield beside the 'fluvius Done' (which rises near Chesterfield). Rotherham is not marked but may be indicated by the house on the bank of the Don between Sheffield and Doncaster. (*from a facsimile published by the Ordnance Survey in 1870*)

The returns state the occupation of many of the male inhabitants, telling us that there were seven tailors, two shoemakers, an ironmonger, three ostelers (innkeepers), two merchants, three drapers, a saddler, a skinner, two cartwrights, five smiths, a mason and two spicers. The presence of a thriving local cloth industry is indicated by the appearance of three fullers, two shearmen, four websters or weavers, a lister (dyer) and a coverlet weaver. If we accept the evidence of surnames, we can add a net maker, another dyer, plumber, ark (chest) maker, brewster, waferer, two gardeners, a swineherd and two butchers. Again on surname evidence, immigrants to the town included people from Wentworth, Dalton, Chesterfield (Dby), Barnsley, Hunshelf, Worksop (Ntt), Badsworth, Retford (Ntt), and two 'walschmen'.

The Wellgate Springs rose in the foreground of this modern view of the street. The overflow from the springs ran down Wellgate and Brookgate (now College Street), which can be seen in the distance. (*Author*)

In Kimberworth there was a resident lord, Lionel Dawtre, knight, and his wife Margaret, assessed at 20s. Below him was John de Wode, franklin (freeholder) who paid 6s 8d. The village had the services of eight smiths, three wrights, a carpenter, a fletcher and two tailors. In Brinsworth John Gunneys, a notary or lawyer who paid 6s 8d, topped the list. The only tradesmen in the township were two smiths. In Greasbrough the list is headed by Robert Mundeshere, merchant, at 12d and there were eight smiths, five wrights, three tailors, a weaver and two fullers. In Dalton everyone paid the basic 4d, except William Hayre, shoemaker, the only tradesman listed, who paid 6d.

3

Largest and Stateliest

The Medieval Church

We know virtually nothing about All Saints' church that stood in Rotherham at the Conquest but it was almost certainly constructed from local stone. It is not known when a more modern Norman church replaced the Saxon structure nor do we know the names of any of the priests who served the church before the early 13th century. The lord of the manor held the advowson, or right of presentation to the living. This was a valuable right for it enabled the lord to make provision for a younger son or to provide for a friend's son.

We have seen in the preceding chapter how the manor of Rotherham became split into two halves. The advowson of the church was also split between the de Vesci and de Tilli families, with each being entitled to appoint a priest. They agreed on a single incumbent and the first recorded rector of Rotherham, Robert de Lexington, was jointly presented to the living by William de Vesci and Geoffrey de Saucensmar in 1227. For the next century or so, however, it was normal for the church to be served by two priests.

When the de Vesci moiety (half share) of the manor was granted to Rufford Abbey, in the 1270s, de Vesci's share of the advowson was included in the grant. John de Lexington had given his share of the manor to Rufford in the mid-1250s. This grant, however, did not include his half share of the advowson. Robert de Lexington, rector of Rotherham, was John's brother. Another brother, Stephen de Lexington, was abbot of the great French abbey of Clairvaux, mother church of the Cistercian order to which Rufford belonged. John gave his share of the advowson to Clairvaux who, in 1256, obtained papal permission to appropriate their moiety. The abbey became rector (taking the great tithes – one tenth of the corn, hay and wool produced in the parish each year), appointing a vicar to

The parish church of All Saints, photographed from Church Street. The structure seen here is basically that erected by Rufford Abbey in the 15th century. (*Author*)

serve the church. For a time, therefore, Rotherham parish church was served by both a rector, for the Rufford half and a vicar, for the Clairvaux half. Clairvaux soon found that administering half a church in distant Yorkshire was more trouble than it was worth and, in 1278, leased its share of the church to Rufford, in return for an annual rent of £20, paying the vicar £5 p.a.

For the next 70 years Rufford appointed both the rector and the vicar to the church. In 1297 the church was valued at £44 13s 4d, made up as follows:

The share of the Abbey of Clairvaux	£16 13s 4d
The vicar of that share	£5 0s 0d
The share of Roger with the vicar of that part	£21 13s 4d
A pension to the Priory of Lewes	£1 6s 8d

The Roger referred to here was Roger de Blyth who had been instituted as rector of the Rufford moiety in 1288. The grant of the de Vesci moiety to Rufford had given them only the right to appoint the rector who took all the tithes, great and small. Roger had obviously chosen to appoint a vicar to assist him. The origin of the pension to Lewes Priory is unclear.

Rufford's control of both halves of the advowson was not unchallenged. In 1314 the archbishop was forbidden to admit anyone to the benefice at Rotherham until a dispute over the advowson between Rufford and Gilbert de Aton, heir to William de Vesci, was settled.

An interior view of the parish church with the early 17th-century pulpit at the corner of the tower arch and the 18th-century organ in the north transept. The pulpit now stands on the other side of the nave. (*Rotherham Central Library*)

This was an attempt by Aton to gain control of the de Vesci share of the church. As late as 1389 Thomas Molde, chaplain, was given royal licence to travel to Rome to pursue a claim concerning the vicarage of Rotherham before the papal court. Unfortunately the substance of the claim and the result of the appeal to Rome have not been recorded.

In 1332 Rufford was able to obtain permission from Edward III to appropriate the rectory of the de Vesci half of the church. It was not until 1349, however, that they were able to obtain the archbishop's agreement, upon payment of an annual pension of 26s 8d to the Archbishop of York and 13s 4d to the Dean and Chapter. This was twice what was usually paid and reflects the relative value of the benefice. The abbey was now able to take the great tithes, appointing a vicar to serve the church. The vicar was to be provided with a house and a generous annual stipend of 25 marks, out of which he was expected to find bread, wine, lights, books and vestments for the church. The abbey was to be responsible for repairing the chancel when necessary. The abbey chose to unite the two halves of the church, and in 1355 John de Fledburgh was appointed by Rufford as the first vicar of the united church.

The house provided for the vicar almost certainly stood in the south-east corner of the churchyard, at the head of Vicarage Lane, on the site occupied by its successors. In 1423 Simon de Mersburgh released to his relative, John de Mersburgh, a house lying between 'the house belonging to St Mary on the west side and the house that formerly belonged to the rector of Rotherham on the east, butting on the churchyard at one end and the high road on the other'. This suggests that the vicar of the de Tilli moiety and the rector of the de Vesci moiety had separate accommodation and that the three properties fronted on to the High Street, although the later vicarage faced on to the churchyard. John de Mersburgh, in 1435, leased the house to Rufford for 17 years, rent free. Possibly the abbey then converted all three dwellings into a single vicarage.

During the Hundred Years War it was not possible to pay Clairvaux's rent to France and the Crown diverted the £20 into its own coffers. Apart from a brief period of peace in the 1360s, the rent was never again paid to Clairvaux. In 1445 Henry VI granted the rent to Henry Beaumont for life, with reversion to King's College, Cambridge, as part of his original endowment of the college. Finally, in 1467, foreign monasteries were forbidden to own property in England and the rent was granted to the Dean and Canons of Windsor. They continued to receive it until 1537.

The church of which Rufford was given a share in the 1250s was little smaller than the present church. Surviving fragments and foundations show that it consisted of a nave with aisles, north and south transepts and chancel with central tower, constructed of local sandstone with limestone dressings. It was 127 ft long with a 64 ft nave and 38 ft chancel. Once they had complete control of the church the monks at Rufford embarked on a modernisation campaign, commencing with the chancel. This they rebuilt in Early English style, with a low roof. The lower courses of the chancel walls date from the late 13th century and the original low roofline can still be traced in the stonework of the crossing tower. Repairs were carried out to the church and tower in 1300. The complete rebuilding of the tower can be dated to the years around 1409, for in that year the Archbishop of York issued an instruction to the townspeople of Rotherham to help the abbot with the work of rebuilding the tower 'from the foundation'. The rebuilding of the nave was probably started before the tower was finished and the whole work was completed by the end of the 15th century, leaving the town with a fine Perpendicular church. The work of rebuilding was

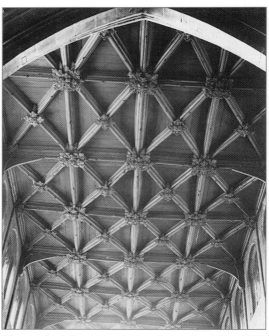

The cambered tie-beam roof of the chancel, dated by Pevsner to 1510–12. (*Rotherham Central Library*)

The roof of the nave, dating from about the 15th century. (*Rotherham Central Library*)

helped by bequests from parishioners. John Bolom left 20 marks towards the fabric of the church in 1435 and in 1452 Robert Lister bequeathed 13s 4d towards making the stalls and the same amount towards paving the church. In rebuilding the nave the cushion capitals of the Norman nave arcade were used as foundations for the new arcade pillars, and can still be seen beneath removable paving stones. Many reused Norman stones can also be found in the walls of the north aisle and the chancel. The clerestory of the chancel was added in 1508–12, with its roof dating from the same period, and Pevsner, in his *The Buildings of England: Yorkshire, West Riding*, also attributes the fan vaulting of the crossing to the early Tudor period and it must therefore be an insertion into the earlier tower. Pevsner describes the church as 'one of the largest and stateliest of the parish churches of Yorkshire', and '. . . far more monumental than such comparable churches as the parish churches of Wakefield and Halifax'. The completed church was 147 ft long with a nave 62 ft wide and a tower and spire 180 ft high.

Because the parish of Rotherham was so large, parishioners in outlying areas (such as Catcliffe and Orgreave) found it difficult to attend services in the parish church. This difficulty was recognised by the establishment of chapels of ease in outlying areas. The foundation of the chapel at Greasbrough is obscure because it was unendowed and does not appear in the chantry lists. More is known about the chapel at Tinsley. In 1549 it was said to have been founded as a chantry chapel by the ancestors of Thomas Wentworth, esquire, and Nicholas Denman the younger, gent., to pray for the souls of the founders, but it may be much older (see Chapter 1). The chantry priest also ministered to the sick folk of Tinsley, Brinsworth, Orgreave and Catcliffe 'at such tyme when the waters be uppe', i.e. when the Don and Rother were in flood. The chapel was said to be 2 miles from the parish church and the priest was required to provide the sacrament to sick inhabitants 'when the waters of Rother and Don are so urgent that the curate of Rotherham cannot to theym repayre, not the inhabitants of Tymnyslaw, Brynsforth, Orgrave and Catclyff to hym, nother on hors back or bote'. These chapels of ease soon gained the right to conduct christenings and burials, but marriages remained reserved for the parish church. In the case of Tinsley, the chapel soon became to all intents and purposes independent of the parish church. The advowson of the chapel at Tinsley was separate from that of Rotherham and in the 14th century it belonged to the de Tynneslowe (or de Tinsley) family, who were lords of the manor as tenants of the Honor of Tickhill.

One of the glories of the medieval parish church in Rotherham was its chantry chapels. Chantries were private chapels within the church with an altar for saying mass for the soul(s) of the founder(s) and of their nominees. The chapel was usually endowed with land to support a priest. There were five chantries within Rotherham parish church. The earliest was founded in 1318 by John Letterd, clerk, of Car House, Greasbrough, a grange or farm of the priory at Monk Bretton, near Barnsley. It was dedicated to Our Lady and became known as 'Our Lady of Car'. This altar was probably situated in the north transept, the roof of which is carved with roses, the emblem of the Virgin Mary. When the property of Monk Bretton Priory was sold by Henry VIII, the purchaser, William Ramsden, was required to pay 73s 4d a year to the chantry priest.

The early Tudor fan vaulting in the tower. (*Rotherham Central Library*)

In 1409 John Grenewode, vicar of Rotherham, Robert Hill, chaplain and John de Palden, a prosperous tanner, paid the Crown 20 marks for a licence to found the Chantry of the Holy Cross for one chaplain, chosen by the vicar, to pray at the altar of the Holy Cross for the good estate of de Palden, Isabel his wife and their souls after death. The altar was an earlier foundation than the chantry, having been founded in 1357 by the Gild of the Holy Cross, a religious fraternity of both men and women offering mutual charitable help. Once a year the brothers and sisters of the Gild assembled in the church to choose a chaplain to say mass and perform other services daily before the cross in the church, and were charged with finding torches and tapers to the value of 13s 4d annually to burn before the cross on feast days. At the Feast of the Exaltation of the Cross (14 September) the Gild came in procession to the church to renew the torches and tapers. The endowments of the Gild included four houses at Morthen, given by Hugh Poneye, and a house and land in Rotherham given by John Bolom. The altar was probably in the north chapel.

Little is known about the Gild of Our Lady, which also had an altar within the church. In 1547 it was said to have been founded by 'divers and well disposed persons of the town of Rotherham' to pray for the souls of the benefactors and all Christian souls. Among the outgoings of this chantry was the duty to provide 5 pecks of rye a year to Tickhill Castle. The origins of the Chantry of St Katherine are similarly obscure. The priest was required to say mass every day at 6 a.m., winter and summer. There was also a gild attached to this chantry with the appointment of 'Greaves [reeves or stewards] for St Katherine's service', being recorded in 1538.

The final chantry within the parish church was the richest and most finely decorated. It was founded by Rotherham's most famous medieval son, Thomas Rotherham, Archbishop of York, and will be dealt with in detail in the next chapter.

4

Bridge, Chapel and College

The Fifteenth Century

We have seen earlier how Rotherham owes its existence, at least in part, to the existence of a ford across the River Don, traces of which were found when the present Chantry Bridge was built in 1930. It is not known when a bridge replaced the ford or whether there was an earlier wooden bridge before the present stone one. We do know that the bridge predates the chapel attached to it and that it was in existence by 1483. The original bridge was 15 ft wide, supported by four pointed arches. In his will, dated 1490, Thomas Webster of Rotherham left 20s towards the making (or repair) of 'the bridge called Rotherbryg'.

Attached to the bridge is Rotherham's best-known landmark, the Chapel on the Bridge. This can be dated to 1483 for in August of that year John Bokyng, grammar teacher, bequeathed 3s 4d 'to the fabric of the chapel to be built on Rotherham Bridge'. An examination of the stonework of the bridge and the chapel shows that the bridge clearly predated the building of the chapel, as the original cutwater extends into the crypt of the chapel.

The Rotherham chapel is one of only four midstream chapels that survive. The others are at Wakefield (WYk), St Ives (Hun) and Bradford on Avon (Wil). Bridge chapels were well patronised by travellers, saying prayers for a safe journey or giving thanks for a safe arrival. The Chapel on the Bridge is solidly built of local sandstone, of two bays with a three-light window in each bay, a four-light window at the east end and a tunnel-vaulted crypt

The underside of Rotherham Bridge, showing the original 15th-century sandstone ribs under the arches. (*Author*)

The Chapel on the Bridge as it is today, following the restoration of 1923. (*Author*)

beneath, reached by a trapdoor. A spiral staircase gave access to a small gallery at the west end. It had no endowment of property or rents to support it, relying on the offerings made by travellers and on support from pious townspeople. Several, in addition to John Bokyng, made bequests to the chapel. In 1484 Margaret Tayliour left 3*s* 4*d* towards the fabric of 'the chapel of the Blessed Mary'. On his death the following year Arnold Reresby of Rotherham left 6*s* 8*d* towards the making or glazing of a window in the 'Chapel of the Blessed Mary on Rotherham Bridge', suggesting that the building was still under construction.

Because of its dedication, the chapel became the centre of a cult of the Virgin Mary. It is also likely that the men known as the Greaves of Our Ladies Lights were connected with the chapel. Guest prints some accounts of these greaves from the reign of Henry VIII, showing them as responsible for money collected from the public and for supplying wax tapers. They were apparently selected annually in pairs on a territorial basis, as there is reference to greaves for Westgate and for Bridgegate. The connection between the greaves and the Chapel on the Bridge is shown by the accounts for 1538 when Thomas Richardson and John Holden recorded that there had been delivered into their hands 'of Our Lady's stock of the Bridge, for certain stuff that was there, in money £6 2*s*'. They were also holding 'an image of Our Lady and her Son, of fine gold, and a broken ring of gold'. In addition they were responsible for the town's stock of armour and weapons. In 1538 this consisted of 'four jacks (leather coats plated with iron), a plate coat, six pairs of splents (armour to protect the elbows), six standards, five sallets (helmets), two sheaves of arrows', in the custody of Robert Walker and Richard Cutler.

The second half of the 15th century was overshadowed by the Wars of the Roses, the struggle for the crown between the Houses of York and Lancaster that began with the Battle of St Albans (1455) and whose last echoes died with the Battle of Stoke (1487). Rotherham played a minor part in this protracted struggle. With an abbey as lord of the manor, there was no great lord attempting to recruit his tenants to whichever party he chose to support. The same was not true of Kimberworth where the lord of the manor was the Earl of Warwick. From the Spencers, Kimberworth had descended to Ann Beauchamp who married

Richard Neville, Earl of Warwick (1428–71). The Earl, better known as Warwick the Kingmaker, was one of the most prominent players in the Wars of the Roses and is likely to have required Kimberworth to supply men, materials and money to support his cause. Initially Warwick was a supporter of the claim of Edward III's great-grandson, Richard Plantagenet, Duke of York, who was married to Warwick's aunt. The king, Henry VI, preferred the claim of Edmund Beaufort, Duke of Somerset, illegitimate grandson of Edward III's son, John of Gaunt. Although Rotherham managed to sit out the war as a relative backwater, it played host to one of the campaigning armies on at least three occasions.

Warwick's capture of the king at the Battle of Northampton on 10 July 1460 opened the way for York to return from Ireland to press his claim to the throne. Somerset, however, crossed from France and raised the Lancastrian supporters in the north. In December York left London and marched north, following the ancient route from London to the West Riding, via Nottinghamshire, and beating off a Lancastrian ambush at Worksop. The army would have passed through Rotherham and possibly even stayed the night and recruited a few local men. On 21 December York reached his stronghold at Sandal Castle, south of Wakefield. On 30 December the two armies met in the Battle of Wakefield, which resulted in the death of the Duke of York and the complete defeat of his army. The Yorkist mantle fell on York's eldest son Edward, Earl of March. The following year saw the defeat of Warwick and release of Henry VI at the second Battle of St Albans (17 February), the seizure of the throne by Edward, Duke of York (as Edward IV) and the bloody rout of the Lancastrians at the Battle of Towton, near Tadcaster (WRY). On this occasion the Yorkist army advanced north from London via Cambridge and the Great North Road, although Rotherham may have suffered the attentions of foraging parties.

No sooner was Edward on the throne than he and his main supporter, Warwick, fell out. Warwick began plotting rebellion with the king's brother George, Duke of Clarence. The Yorkist army was defeated by the rebels at Edgecote Moor (26 July 1469) and the king was taken into Warwick's 'protection'. Edward was able to escape and in March 1470 routed an army of Warwick's and Clarence's supporters near Stamford (Lin). Warwick and Clarence were then at Coventry. Warwick pretended to submit to Edward's instructions to disband his army and meet him at Stamford, but wrote to his Yorkshire supporters to meet him at Rotherham with all the men they could muster. He then marched via Derby to Chesterfield (Dby). The King meanwhile moved to Doncaster. Warwick reached Rotherham to find only a handful of supporters awaiting him and marched on into Lancashire. Unable to raise any support there, he and Clarence fled to France. Warwick now offered his services to the House of Lancaster and invaded England in September 1470. Edward was in York, dealing with uprisings in the north. He hurried south, stopping for the night in Doncaster and dispersing his men into billets in the surrounding villages. Here he heard that John Neville, Marquis of Montagu, who was gathering an army on the King's orders and who was due to meet Edward at Rotherham on the following day, had declared for Henry VI and was advancing on Doncaster. Unable to gather his scattered army, Edward fled to the Continent. Warwick entered London and released Henry VI from the Tower. In the Low Countries Edward recruited an army of Burgundian mercenaries and landed at Ravenspur, near Hull. He marched south via Doncaster and Nottingham and entered London on 11 April, taking Henry VI prisoner once more. As Warwick advanced on the capital from the Midlands, Edward advanced to meet him at Barnet. The resulting battle led to the defeat of the Lancastrians and the death of Warwick. Following the defeat of a Lancastrian army raised by Henry VI's queen, Margaret of Anjou, at Tewkesbury (Gls) and the death of their son, Edward, Prince of Wales, Henry VI was quietly put to death in the Tower and Edward IV was undisputed King of England.

With the death of Warwick, the lordship of Kimberworth passed to his daughter, Ann Neville. She had been married to Edward IV's younger brother, Richard, Duke of Gloucester in 1472. When Richard succeeded in ousting his brother's children and seized the throne in 1483 as Richard III, the manor became a royal possession and it remained in the hands of the Crown after Henry Tudor defeated Richard at the Battle of Bosworth (1485) to take the throne as Henry VII. Henry's throne was initially far from secure. In 1487 Henry's opponents raised up the son of an Oxford joiner, Lambert Simnel, as the 'true' Earl of Warwick escaped from the Tower. In May Simnel was crowned Edward VI in Dublin and in June the rebels landed in Lancashire. Marching into Yorkshire they advanced south via Castleford towards Rotherham which was reached on 13 June. Three days later the two armies met at East Stoke, south of Newark (Ntt), the battle resulting in the rout of the rebels. Simnel was captured, but his life was spared and he was put to work in the royal kitchen.

The triumph of Edward IV was to have a profound effect on the career of one son of Rotherham. Thomas Rotherham, also known as Thomas Scot, was born in Rotherham on St Bartholomew's Day (24 August) 1423, the son of Thomas and Alice Rotherham alias Scot. This child was to die in 1500 as Archbishop of York, having participated in the momentous events of the second half of the century at the highest level.

The dual surname 'Rotherham alias Scot' has long puzzled historians and has given rise to a number of explanations. What is certain is that the family was closely related to the Scott family of Barnes Hall, Ecclesfield. In his will, made in 1498, the Archbishop left the manor of Barnes Hall, which he had purchased from Robert Shatton in 1476, to his kinsman John Scott together with the manor of Howsleys which he had purchased from Sir Thomas Wortley. In the event of John dying without heirs, both were to pass to John's brother, Richard Scott. Thomas Rotherham bore the same arms, three bucks trippant, attired or, as did the Scotts of Barnes Hall. In every contemporary reference to the Archbishop and in every document that he himself wrote, he is referred to as Rotherham and both his brothers were known as Rotherham. The simple answer to the name confusion is that Scott was probably his mother's name.

In both his will and the statutes of the College of Jesus, Thomas Rotherham records his birth in Rotherham and his baptism in the parish church. We know that St Bartholomew's Day was his birthday because he tells us in his will. He had two brothers, John and Roger, and a sister whose name is unknown. The most momentous event in his early life was the arrival in the town of: 'a teacher of grammar who came to Rotherham by I know not what fate but I believe that it was by the grace of God he came thither, who taught me and other youths, whereof others with me reached higher stations. . . .'

The wording of Rotherham's will suggests that both his family home and the house occupied by this teacher were close together on the site later occupied by the College of Jesus. When he had learned all he could from this teacher, Rotherham would almost certainly have been sent to a school elsewhere to continue his education. It has been suggested that this school was Eton. Henry VI did not found Eton until 1440 when Rotherham was 17 and the school buildings were only partly completed by 1443 when Thomas became one of the earliest scholars admitted to King's College, Cambridge. When

Rotherham first went up there were only twelve scholars and servants and choristers in the college, and its buildings were incomplete. He remained at Cambridge until 1458, during which period he took his degree and entered the priesthood.

Rotherham's first appointment outside Cambridge was as provost of the collegiate church at Wingham, near Canterbury, in 1458. At the same period he was also appointed chaplain to the Earl of Oxford. This would have brought him into contact with the Court where Oxford was one of the strongest Lancastrian supporters. Rotherham may perhaps have been called on to act as chaplain to Oxford one final time before the earl's execution in 1462 following the Lancastrian defeat at Towton and Edward IV's coronation. The fall of his patron did not put a stop to Rotherham's advancement. In 1461 he had been appointed to the rectory of Ripple (Wor) and in 1465 he became Prebend of Welton Brinkhall within Lincoln Cathedral. As early as 1465 the king had recommended Thomas to the Pope to replace the ailing John Low as Bishop of Rochester (Ken). In 1467 he took the first step in a parallel career in politics when Edward IV made him Keeper of the Privy Seal and his personal chaplain. The following year saw his consecration as Bishop of Rochester and his choice by Edward as ambassador to the French king. When Warwick turned kingmaker again to restore Henry VI in 1470, Rotherham retired from public life to emerge after the defeat and death of Warwick the following year. February 1471 saw him employed as ambassador to the court of Burgundy and in March he was promoted to the much larger see of Lincoln. In 1474 he exchanged the office of Keeper of the Privy Seal for the far greater office of Chancellor. As well as being head of the judicial system, the Chancellor was keeper of the

This portrait of Archbishop Thomas Rotherham is based on a 17th-century portrait which may not be accurate. (*Rotherham Central Library*)

Dame Alice Scot, mother of Archbishop Rotherham, from her brass in the Wenlock Chapel, Luton parish church, 1491. (*Rotherham Central Library*)

Great Seal and one of the chief advisors to the Crown. In this capacity he accompanied the king on his abortive invasion of France in 1475. Five years later he returned to his native county as Archbishop of York although his duties as Chancellor must have kept him away from York for much of the time. He was heavily involved with the ceremony that surrounded the funeral of Edward IV in April 1483. Shortly after the young Edward V entered London, under the close 'protection' and control of his uncle Richard, Duke of Gloucester, Rotherham was relieved of the office of Chancellor and he was committed to the Tower, where he remained until after Richard III's coronation on 6 July. He never again attained his previous eminence in public affairs.

In 1471 Rotherham had been granted the manor of Luton (Bed) and the other Bedfordshire and Hertfordshire estates of John, Lord Wenlock, one of the chief supporters of the Earl of Warwick after his defection to the Lancastrian cause. The Luton estate included the newly built brick house called Someries, and here Rotherham installed his brother John Rotherham and family, together with their widowed mother. In 1474 Edward IV and Thomas Rotherham, together with Rotherham's brother and mother, founded a religious gild of the Holy Trinity in connection with Luton church. The first register of the Luton Guild still survives. The frontispiece is a magnificent illumination showing the Holy Trinity enthroned. Kneeling in front is Thomas Rotherham in his bishop's robes, flanked by the king and queen and the king's mother. Other people portrayed are thought to include John Rotherham, their younger brother, Dr Roger Rotherham, and their mother. This is the only contemporary portrait of Thomas Rotherham.

Towards the end of his time as Bishop of Lincoln, Thomas turned his mind towards leaving some permanent reminder of his connection with his home town. On 28 July 1480 he purchased a licence from Edward IV to found a chantry within the parish church empowering him to 'make, found, erect, create and establish . . . a certain perpetual chantry with one chaplain who shall for ever celebrate divine service every day at the altar within the parochial church of Rotherham . . . by that Bishop newly constructed, built and dedicated to the glory, praise, and honour of Our Lord Jesus Christ. . . .'

The College Inn, College Street, which incorporated much of the structure of the south wing of the College of Jesus. It is shown here decorated for the visit of the Prince of Wales (later Edward VII) to open Clifton Park in 1891. (*Rotherham Central Library*)

The chantry was to be founded for the souls of the king and queen, of their son Edward, Prince of Wales, and the rest of their children, and of the bishop, his friends and benefactors. Rotherham was empowered to endow the chantry with estates to the value of £20 per year. Hunter believed that the chantry was never founded, being absorbed into Rotherham's greater design of the College of Jesus. It is clear from the wording of the licence, however, that Rotherham had already created the Chapel of Jesus within the parish church. This chapel was constructed in the angle between the south transept and the chancel. Carved on the roof bosses of the chapel are the five wounds of Christ, the monogram of Our Lady, the wheel of St Katherine and the Sun in Glory, emblem of the House of York. During the restoration of 1873 traces of blue paint and gold stars were found on the roof panels.

The wording of the licence also suggests that the bishop had already formed the intention to found a college in Rotherham, for part of the purpose of the proposed chantry was 'for certain works of piety and mercy according to ordinances, statutes and constitutions to be made, ordained and established by that said bishop'. The intention to found a college in his home town seems to have come to him after 1475, for his earliest surviving will, made that year, makes no mention of a college or of any property in Rotherham. It is likely that it was the subsequent death of his mother and his inheritance of the family estate in Rotherham coupled with his translation to the richer diocese of York that gave him the chance to achieve his ambition. On 22 January 1483 he purchased a royal licence to found a college at Rotherham with a provost and two fellows, one of whom was to be a master of grammar and the other a teacher of song. The scope of the college could be extended in the future if increased income were to make it possible. The foundation deed for the college was executed by Rotherham on 8 February 1483.

The statutes that Rotherham drafted explained his reasons for establishing the College of Jesus:

- Gratitude to the anonymous teacher of grammar who had started him on the road to education and advancement.
- The wish to establish a school of singing to provide choristers for the parish church, as even the many simple country people who flocked to the church could understand music. He therefore established a 'man learned in singing and six choristers or chapel boys, so that divine service may be celebrated there the more honourably for ever'.
- The desire to provide a teacher 'skilled and learned in the art of writing and reckoning' to instruct the 'many youths endowed with the light and shrewdness of nature, but all do not attain the dignity and height of priesthood, as such are fitted rather for the mechanical arts and other worldly affairs.'
- The provision of housing for the various chantry priests within the parish church, who were reported to be 'eating and passing the night in different places, to the scandal of themselves and of the church' and to 'have been given up to ease and idleness'.

We can see from this that Rotherham had found the means to increase the establishment from two fellows to three, headed by a provost who 'must be a priest, doctor in sacred theology, or at least a bachelor of the same, of the University of Cambridge, of praiseworthy life and good and approved conversation'. His salary was set at 20 marks (£13 6s 8d), while the fellows of grammar and singing received 10 marks each and the fellow in writing 8 marks (£5 6s 8d). The fellows were to have individual rooms but were to dine together daily.

The Provost was to pay the college servants, for the fuel for the kitchen and common room, and for salt, salt fish, flour and candles. Neither the provost nor any of the fellows were allowed to accept any benefice requiring residence away from Rotherham. Every year the Provost was to provide, at the cost of the college, woollen cloth 'of a convenient colour', for gowns for the fellows and the six college boys. In 1495 the fellows' gowns were described as being red, blue, violet, green and russet.

The provost and fellows were assigned prominent places on the left side of the parish church choir, where they were to attend on every church feast at morning mass and vespers. Rotherham intended his college to be independent of the parish church and the provost and fellows were specifically exempted from 'the precepts and mandates' of Rufford Abbey and the vicar. They were, however, required to celebrate masses at least twice a week in the Chapel of Jesus in the parish church, to include specified collects, including prayers for the soul of Thomas Rotherham, his parents and Edward IV.

The provost was to choose six 'of the poorer boys of these parts, of the fitter and apter at learning and virtue' from the parishes of Rotherham and Ecclesfield, to be provided with food and clothing and taught singing, grammar and writing up to the age of 18. They were to act as servers during mass and to wait on the provost and fellows at table. The singing master and his pupils were kept busy singing the Mass of Jesus before the altar of Jesus every Friday, with an antiphon of Jesus at vespers, an antiphon of the Blessed Mary every Saturday at her altar in the parish church and, on the eves of every feast of the Blessed Mary, an antiphon for her at the altar in the Chapel on the Bridge. The custom arose of the six choristers electing one of their number as the 'boy-bishop' from St Nicholas Day (6 December) to Holy Innocents Day (28 December). The chosen boy wore a mitre and episcopal vestments, preached a sermon and sang the service. During this period the choristers occupied the higher choir stalls, with the provost and fellows in the lower stalls.

The inhabitants of the college were forbidden to play games 'prohibited to the clergy by right', nor were they to 'frequent taverns or suspected houses or disgraceful shows'. They were especially to shun 'the weakness of the flesh and its uncleanness and dishonour', and no woman 'of any condition or state' was permitted to remain the night within the college 'without a great reason'.

The timber-framed north wing of the College, photographed during demolition in 1868. (*Rotherham Central Library*)

A well on the college site, found during excavations during the extension to Woolworths, *c.* 1958. (*Rotherham Central Library*)

We know from the archbishop's will that the foundation stone of the college was laid on St Gregory's Day (12 May) 1483. The buildings were still unfinished when the archbishop made his final will in 1598. The royal licence describes the site of the college as 'a certain ground or site of the said Archbishop . . . which said ground contains in length between the waste land of the Abbot of Rufford from the east part and the tenement of John Wentworth on the west part 638 ft 7 in and in breadth between the close of the said Abbot called the Imp-yard on the north and the common stream of Rotherham . . . running and falling into the water of the Don on the south, 623 ft 6 in.' These dimensions equate roughly to the distance from the bottom of College Lane to the bridge approach. The site was further increased by taking the 'Imp-yard' (nursery) on lease from the abbot, extending the grounds down to the Don.

The college was constructed of red brick, possibly the first use of brick in the town. Guest, writing in 1879, could remember that part of the surrounding wall still stood to 12 ft high as recently as 1860. The buildings were arranged around a quadrangle with a thick, heavy wall, topped with coping stones 3 or 4 ft across, and pierced by the main entrance gates on the College Street frontage. The college consisted of a mansion house roofed in stone slates, with a garden and orchard containing 2 acres, another house where the schools were held and a gatehouse 6 yd by 4 yd with two turrets. To the east of the gate house was the chapel, 18 yd by 10 yd with a crested roof and to the west was a chamber 12 yd by 10 yd. The gatehouse, chapel and chamber were roofed in lead. The one remaining visible fragment of the college, the doorway that was relocated to Boston park in 1876, has been dated to the 16th century on stylistic grounds, and probably dates from the secularisation of the site after 1547.

Rotherham endowed his creation with a considerable estate for its support, and others were to add to it during the 64 years of its existence. The main endowments from the Archbishop were the churches at Almondbury (WRY) and Laxton (Ntt), worth together £41 a year, with other property in and around Rotherham. An early addition was the bequest by John Bokyng, grammar master (d. 1483), of land worth 8s a year after the death of his wife. In 1547 the

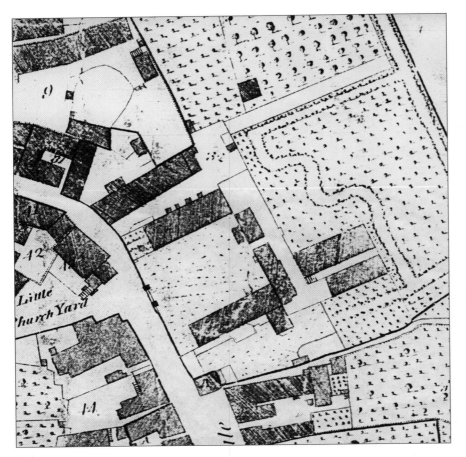

The college
buildings with
surrounding
gardens, as they
survived in 1774.
The main buildings
lay around the
quadrangle facing
on to College Street
(*Rotherham Central
Library*)

college estates were valued at £130 16s 1d and included houses and land in Rotherham, Kimberworth, Masbrough, Dalton, Thorpe Hesley, Scholes, Greasbrough, Mexborough, Bramwith, Wentworth, Fishlake, Almondbury and Beighton (Dby).

The first provost was Thomas Graybarn, rector of Sherington (Bucks) which he exchanged in 1486 for the rectory of Handsworth. As rector he would have been able to appoint a vicar to care for these parishes, as his job as provost required him to live in Rotherham. The first two fellows were Edmund Carter and William Alyson. The third fellowship was reserved for the priest of St Katherine's Chantry as Rotherham felt that this was under-endowed. Greybarn resigned in 1501 and died shortly afterwards, asking to be buried in the Jesus Choir. He left 6s 8d to the bells of Rotherham parish church, 3s 4d to the upkeep of Rotherham Bridge and the residue of his estate to the exhibition of poor scholars at the grammar school and at university. William Rawson, who died in 1495, described himself as Provost of the College of Jesus in his will dated 1495, but no appointment of Rawson appears in the Archbishop's register. Guest suggests that Greybarn must have resigned and then been reappointed after Rawson's death. Rawson also wanted to be buried in the Jesus Chapel. The instructions for his funeral were elaborate and included money for 12 poor torchbearers, bread and beer for a wake and dinner in the college.

5

'A Meatfull Large Town'

Tudor Rotherham

At the close of the 15th century the town of Rotherham had a fine parish church in the latest style and the College of Jesus was the envy of the surrounding towns, as was the standard of singing in the church. The first cloud on the horizon arrived with the death of the town's greatest benefactor. Thomas Rotherham, Archbishop of York, died on 29 May 1500 at his house at Cawood (WRY) and was buried in a vault beneath the marble tomb he had already prepared to the north of the altar of the Blessed Mary in York Minster. The tomb, badly damaged by fire in 1829, was restored in 1832 at the cost of the Rector and Fellows of Lincoln College, Oxford. When it was opened in 1735 the bones of the archbishop were said to have 'nothing remarkable about them' although the vault did contain a carved wooden head. It is unclear whether this was intended to be a representation of the archbishop, possibly used during his funeral.

Thomas Rotherham's final will, finished on his birthday 24 August 1498, is far longer and more elaborate that of 1475. After commending his soul to God, and relating his birth and baptism in Rotherham, he relates the foundation of the College of Jesus 'which I have

Archbishop Rotherham's tomb in York Minster. (*Rotherham Central Library*)

begun to rear'. The endowment of the college with the churches of Laxton (Ntt) and Almondbury (WRY) is confirmed. In the years since the foundation he had increased the endowment to include his manors of Barkway (Hrt), Sharpness (Glo), Sibthorp (Ntt), Hawksworth (Ntt), and Weston (Ntt), together with various lands, houses and rents in Rotherham, Greasbrough, Thorpe Hesley, Scholes, Brinsworth, Dinnington, Throapham, Gildingwells, Mexborough, Hatfield, Wentworth and elsewhere. The total annual value of these estates was £92 11s 8½d. He also bequeathed a large quantity of plate, minutely described in the will, including cups 'with a sun worked in the bottom of each'. These were possibly gifts from Edward IV whose emblem was the sun. The provost and fellows received rich sets of vestments, including one of red purple velvet worked with golden flowers and another with an image of St Katherine on the back. He also bequeathed a mitre of cloth of gold for use by the boy-bishop. The college chapel received two beautiful illuminated missals, one after the practice used at York and the other after the use at Salisbury. The needs of the choristers were provided by the gift of two new 'large and beautiful' antiphonaries and two 'new and beautiful' graduals. To York Minster he left a 'more worthy mitre' which had cost him 500 marks (£333 6s 8d). He left £200 as a defence fund for the College of Jesus, in case it ever became embroiled in litigation. His final request was that 1,000 masses be said for his soul, so that his soul 'may be more mildly dealt with'.

Even after the archbishop's death the college and the parish church continued to be the recipients of gifts and bequests. Among the greatest benefactors was Henry Carnebull, Archdeacon of York, and a great friend of Thomas Rotherham. In 1505 he obtained a licence to found a chantry at the altar of Jesus in the parish church to pray for his own soul, the soul of Thomas Rotherham and the souls of Henry VII, Queen Elizabeth and his mother. This was in addition to the existing chantry priest, and the chantry became known as the Chantry of Jesus and the Blessed Virgin Mary. This was the most richly endowed of the chantries in the parish church. The patronage of this chantry was given to the provost and fellows of the College of Jesus. During a visit to the college during the summer of 1512 Carnebull was taken ill, and died on 10 August, desiring to be buried before the altar in the Chapel of Jesus. His bequests to the chapel included a crucifix supported by the Virgin Mary and St John and two enamelled and parcel gilt (partially gilded) candlesticks.

The years 1508–12 saw the completion of the rebuilding of the parish church with the raising of the chancel roof and the insertion of the clerestory windows. Among the roof bosses can be found the Holy Monogram, the cypher of the Virgin Mary, the initials HC (Henry Carnebull), the initials TB (Thomas Bilton, Abbot of Rufford) and HOTON (Richard Hoton, Provost of the College of Jesus 1502–9 and Vicar of Rotherham 1513–14).

Rufford Abbey, with an annual income of less than £200, was among the earliest abbeys to be dissolved by Henry VIII, the last abbot, Thomas Doncaster, surrendering the abbey to the king's commissioners in 1536. The seizure was excused by allegations of sodomy against six of the monks and of multiple adultery against the abbot. A full inventory of the abbey estates was taken which reveals the importance of Rotherham in abbey affairs. There is a detailed list of the rents received from Rotherham which shows an annual income of £143 8s 3½d. After allowing for charges, the clear income from the town and parish church was £100 0s 7d out of a total abbey income of £176.

The abbey rental tells us that there were at least five forges in the town, one of them in the market-place and one near the church stile, a stone quarry and bakeries in Doncaster Gate, Westgate and Bridgegate. Not all rents were paid in cash. Thomas Hobson was paying

3s 4d and 1 lb of pepper for a tenement in Bridgegate and Alexander Oke was leasing the sub-manor of Eastwood for 114s 8d and eight quarters of oats. Among the more prominent tenants were the Earl of Shrewsbury, the Oke family, Thomas Wentworth of Wentworth, Sir William Fitzwilliam and Mr Mounteney. There is also reference to a hall at Masbrough, tenanted by William Whitmore (the abbey's bailiff) and Edward Blyton. The income from the manor courts had been leased to the bailiff for £4 a year. The rent roll also refers to the Chapel of St James that stood in Wellgate. It must have been out of use by the Dissolution for it was leased to Mr Savage for 13s 4d.

Robert Swift's memorial brass in the parish church. The brass has been inserted into a 14th-century tomb. (*Rotherham Central Library*)

The name that appears most frequently in the accounts is Robert Swift, a prosperous mercer, whose memorial brass in the parish church shows him clad in a long, fur-trimmed gown, kneeling at a desk, with his first wife Anne at an adjoining desk. Their sons, Robert and William, and their daughters, Ann and Margaret, flank them. The inscription tells us that the couple lived many years in the town 'in vertuus fame, grett wellthe and good woorship'. His eldest son, Robert, died in 1558. William Swift's son and grandson were both knighted and his great-grandson, Barnham Swift, was created Viscount Carlingford in 1627. In the Rufford accounts, Robert Swift was leasing the town corn mill, the rectory and several other properties, including tenements in Bridgegate, Westgate, and the forge in the market-place. Altogether he was paying the abbey £85 10s 9d every year, almost 60 per cent of their Rotherham income.

In 1537 Henry VIII granted the site of Rufford Abbey, the manor of Rufford and all the other abbey estates, including the manor and rectory of Rotherham, to George Talbot, Earl of Shrewsbury. He already held the manor and castle of Sheffield, so Rotherham was a logical extension of his estates. The earl did not enjoy the new estates for long as he died on 26 July 1538, being succeeded by his son Francis. The Talbots already held some estates in Rotherham, including a 'chief house' in Westgate, most likely inhabited by his Rotherham agent. Guest states that this house was still standing in the early part of the 18th century and occupied a street frontage of almost 60 ft.

Some manor court rolls for the early years of the Shrewsbury lordship (1537–53) have survived in the Brotherton Library, Leeds, and give a good idea of the routine business transacted by the manor court. The court held on 30 September 1551 laid down a series of byelaws for the manorial tenants, showing the court's concern for the regulation of the grazing on the commons, the maintenance of a clean water supply, not leaving carts in the streets overnight and serious worries about keeping other people's servants in one's house overnight. The fines imposed by the same court covered keeping cattle on the common before Lammas Day (1 August), mowing balks (the unploughed strips of land between the furlongs in the open fields), 'overpressing the commons' (keeping too many beasts) and breaking the pinfold. Guest has preserved accounts for 1578 and 1583 of the 'byerlaw men' who were appointed to enforce the regulations about the keeping of stock. These include many fines for tethering horses among haycocks and corn stacks, cattle straying into the fields, driving sheep across the fallow fields, grazing horses on the common when no common rights were held and giving the pinder (a person responsible for impounding straying animals) 'evyll words'.

The earl's tenants were obliged to grind their corn at the manorial mills on the Don, a jealously guarded right. In 1546 a pain of 13s 4d was laid upon every tenant who took their corn out of the town for grinding. Tenants were equally forbidden to do their own grinding with hand querns. On the other hand, Swyft, the miller, was fined 10s for grinding the corn of outsiders before that of the townspeople. Accounts for the Rotherham mill for the years 1578–82 survive in the British Library and for 1583–9 among the Arundel Castle Muniments in Sheffield Archives. The mills were sufficiently profitable for the earl to be able to lease them to John Pickering and Edward Poppellwell for £160 a year, the tenants being responsible for all repairs. The mills were referred to in the plural because there were two sets of stones, one to grind grain and the other malt.

The Earl of Shrewsbury also acquired the manor of Kimberworth that had fallen into the hands of the Crown. The Crown sold the grange of Monk Bretton Priory at Car House, Greasbrough, in 1545 to William Ramsden, with much other property in Yorkshire and Northamptonshire. The grange property in Greasbrough and Rotherham was valued at 59s 8d but was charged with paying 73s 4d yearly to the chantry priest of our Lady of Car within the parish church. In 1577 that part of Greasbrough that had been part of the Honour of Tickhill and had been held for many years by the Barbot family, was in the hands of Thomas Wentworth of Wentworth.

It was about this time that Rotherham was visited by Henry VIII's antiquary John Leland on his journey round Yorkshire. His is the first written description of the town. Leland entered the town from Pontefract, via the Dearne Valley. His account reads:

from Tarne (Dearne) to Rotherham a iiii miles.
    I enterid into Rotherham by a fair Stone Bridge of iiii Arches and on hit a Chapel of Stone wel wrought.
    Rotherham is a meatfull large Market Town, and hath a large and fair Collegiate Church. The College was institutid by one Scott, Archbisshop of York, otherwise caullid Rotherham, even in the same Place wher now is a very fair College sumptuusly buildid of Brike for a Provost, v Prestes, a Schole-Master of Song and vi Chorestes, a Schole-Master in Grammar and a nother in Writinge.
    Though betwixt Cawoode and Rotherham be good plenti of Wood, yet People burne much Yerth Cole, bycawse hit is plentifully found ther, and sold good chepe.
    A mile from Rotherham be veri good Pittes of Cole.
    In Rotherham be very good Smithes for all cutting tools.

From Rotherham Leland moved on to Worksop (Ntt), and makes only a passing reference to Sheffield as the site of the Earl of Shrewsbury's castle and the chief market of Hallamshire.

In 1539 one of the first tasks of the Earl of Shrewsbury as lay rector was to appoint a new vicar. His choice fell on Simon Clerkson, the last Carmelite prior in York, who had

The former Three Cranes on the High Street is the only surviving timber-framed structure left in the town. The building has stood empty for many years. (*Author*)

embraced Protestant teachings and gained a widespread reputation as a preacher. On 27 October 1541 he obtained a licence of nonresidence, allowing absence from Rotherham for 10 years so that he could 'preach and set forth the Word and the Gospel of God through our said kingdom in Latin sermon or the vulgar tongue' while receiving the 'fruits, rents and profits' of the vicarage. He was required to return to Rotherham to preach four times a year. Clerkson took the opportunity afforded by the new religion to marry, and was therefore deprived of his livings in 1554, after the reversion to Catholicism during Mary's reign.

The inhabitants of Rotherham had barely 10 years to accustom themselves to a secular lord of the manor before they received an even greater shock to their system. The government of Edward VI completed the work begun by his father and abolished chantry chapels. The Chantries Act of 1547 called for the dissolution of all chantries and colleges that still supported the idea of purgatory, to enable the king to provide for the poor, augment the income of vicarages, pay the salaries of preachers and endow free schools. The chantry chapels within the parish church, together with the Chapel on the Bridge and the College of Jesus all fell under the act. Many chantry priests, when they saw that the Act was imminent, chose to alienate part of their estate to local landowners in return for a fixed annual rent. The Crown's commissioners descended on the town to document the chantries' endowments and possessions prior to seizure on behalf of the king. They were particularly concerned to track down any 'concealed lands'. The people of Rotherham were able to conceal the money left by John Reresby for his obit (obituary services), which, as an endowment for superstitious uses, would have been subject to confiscation. As with the monasteries, the property endowments were soon sold off to swell the Exchequer. Two sets of certificates returned by the commissioners in 1549 survive giving details of the chantries.

Within the parish church, the Chantry of Jesus and Our Lady was served by Thomas Pilley, aged 64, and William Feldishend, 30, 'somewhat learned', who received a stipend of £6 13s 4d (the other set of certificates give Thomas Bayshawe as the second priest). The chantry's plate amounted to 47½ oz (or £17 14s 6d) and the endowments brought in £13 6s 8d a year. Thomas Holden, 46, was priest of the Holy Cross, and lived off the proceeds of the endowments worth £10 7s 5d. The plate weighed only 14 oz (or £4). Sixty-year-old

The Chapel on the Bridge showing the bricked-up windows and chimneys inserted after the suppression of the Chapel. (*Rotherham Central Library*)

John Hill was serving the Altar of Our Lady with endowment income of £6 11s 8d and no plate. An ex-monk, Richard Lynge alias Allerton, formerly infirmarer at Rievaulx, had become the priest of St Katherine, receiving a pension of 111s 3d from the Crown in addition to the chantry income of £6 0s 8d. There was 13¾ oz of plate (£3). The Chantry of Our Lady of Carr had no plate and the priest, George Page, 68, relied on the endowment income of £4 6s 8d. After allowing for expenses, the total annual profit of the five chantries, and thus the potential profit to the Crown, was reckoned as either £28 11s 8d plus 73¾ oz plate or £27 6s 6½d plus £22 13s 6d worth of plate. The parish church must have looked a much duller place after the chantry altars had been stripped of all their finery.

Elsewhere in the parish church the rood loft was removed along with the high altar. The parish clerk William Ingram was paid to write out a new version of the service books, the old papist volumes having been taken to York and destroyed. John Kynder and another clerk were paid 2s 8d for writing the 'Book of the Communion' while William Ingram wrote the Book of 'Statutes'. Robert Bate and Thomas Daweson were paid for taking down the high altar and John Yole, Robert Sheppard and another demolished the 'tabernacle' (a canopied niche for the elements of the Mass). The high altar had to be rebuilt when Henry VIII's daughter, Mary, ascended to the throne in 1553 and Catholic worship was restored. The Chapel on the Bridge had no endowments to be seized as it relied on offerings. All the fittings were ripped out, including the golden statue of the Virgin and Child, the tracery was knocked out of the windows and the building was left in a semi-ruined state.

The greatest shock to the town must have been the closure and spoliation of the College of Jesus, which was far more profitable to the Crown than the closure of the chantries. Again there are two sets of valuations, giving differing figures. The first valuation assesses the annual value of the freehold endowments at £130 16s 1¼d. Allowing for £7 19s 7¾d expenses, there was a clear annual profit of £122 16s 5½d. In addition there were goods valued at £31 10s and a considerable amount of plate: 17½ oz gilt, 520½ oz parcel gilt and 23¾ oz silver. The second valuation assesses the endowment income as £127 7s 6d, less £20 2s 1¼d expenses, giving profit of £107 5s 5d. Additionally there were goods valued at £54 7s 8d and plate worth £247 0s 4d.

The last Provost of the College was Robert Pursglove, suffragan Bishop of Hull. Pursglove was in receipt of a stipend of £13 6s 8d in addition to his royal pension of 250 marks

(£166 13s 4d), as a former Prior of Guisborough (NYk), and a further £58 a year from his prebend of Wistow. At the college he also received 18s worth of cloth for his gown, wood and coal for his chamber and an allowance for three horses. After the dissolution of the College, he became rector of his home parish of Tideswell (Dby) and Archdeacon of Nottingham, but lost all preferments on the accession of Elizabeth when he refused to take the oath of supremacy. He lived the rest of his life in retirement, founding a grammar school at Tideswell where he is commemorated by an elaborate brass in the church.

The commissioners thought well of the 36-year-old grammar master, Thomas Snell, described as 'of honest conversation, qualities and learning' and the best paid of the fellows, at £10 a year. Robert Cade, 38, the Singing Master, received £6 13s 4d and John Addy, 61, the Writing Master, had only £5 6s 8d. All three received 12s each for their gowns, 3s 4d for heating their chambers and free barbering and laundry. The free meat, drink and clothing accorded to the choristers and other scholars were valued at 66s 8d each.

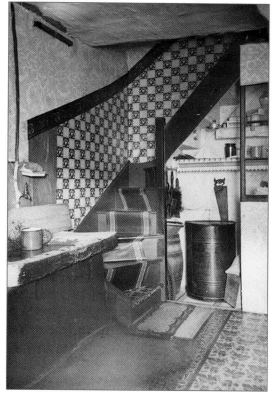

The interior of the Chapel on the Bridge in its last days as a tobacconist's shop. The stairs in the corner led to the upper floor, inserted when the building was converted into almshouses. (*Rotherham Central Library*)

The Earl of Shrewsbury took advantage of the opportunity offered by the dissolution of the college to acquire the site. He already owned the adjoining 'Imp Yard' that had been leased from him by the college since the fall of Rufford. The exact use to which the buildings were put in their early years of secular use is uncertain. Guest quotes a manuscript written in *c.* 1590 by Michael Sherbrook, rector of Wickersley, bemoaning the state of the college buildings:

Now you shall hear of the fate of the College standing in Rotherham, within three miles where I was born and now do dwell; for I learned at the . . . Free School founded by the founder of the College . . . which is a fair house yet standing; but God knoweth how long it shall stand; for certain brick chimneys and other brick walls is decayed and fallen down for lack of use; for there hath been few persons, and sometimes none at all, for a long time dwelling therein. All the lands and possessions are sold from it by the King, saving the yard, Orchard and garden places lying within the Walls thereof; for it is walled with a brick wall. The founding whereof was not to make a malthouse, as it is now used. . . .

The southern wing of the college was incorporated in the College Inn, which included much medieval brickwork in its structure.

The king's commissioners recommended that Thomas Snell be retained as master of the grammar school at a yearly salary of £10 15s 4d payable by the Receiver of the Court of Augmentations. This was paid regularly until 1555, during the reign of Queen Mary, when the receiver refused to pay it. The town seems to have taken on the burden of supporting the school until the change of regime with the accession of Queen Elizabeth. Snell applied successfully for the resumption of his salary, and on 15 April 1561 royal letters patent were issued ordering the recommencement of the payment. The legal costs of the action were borne by the townspeople of Rotherham, who no doubt considered it money well spent. By 1583 the school had been moved into a 'sorry house' on the south side of Jesus Gate close to the manorial bakehouse, allegedly because the Earl of Shrewsbury wished to build a cock pit on the college site. The most prominent scholar of the grammar school in the later 16th century was Robert Sanderson, whose father lived at Guilthwaite Hall, Whiston. Sanderson entered the Church, he rose to be chaplain to Charles I, was appointed Regius Professor of Divinity at Oxford and in October 1660 was consecrated as Bishop of Lincoln. He died in 1663.

Out of the despoliation of the chantry chapels there arose a body of men who were to play an important part in the history of the town for the next 300 years. The feoffees of the Common Lands of Rotherham still exist as a charity, but from the 16th century to the mid-19th century, together with the manor court and the parish officers, they were the nearest that the town had to local government. The feoffees were (and are) headed by a greave, a word that derives from the same root as 'reeve'. The earliest reference to feoffees is in the will of Sir Thomas Reresby (1514), who appointed six feoffees (Robert West, William Swift, Richard Oke, William Oke, Roger Hardy and Robert Brownhill) to supervise the expenditure of an annual rent of 23s 4d from lands at Denaby, half of which was to be spent on an annual obit in the parish church for the repose of his soul and half on 'the common profitt and nedes of the Comons (i.e. common people) of Rotherham'. The first recorded greaves are Robert Swift and William Whitmore, referred to as 'common greaves' in accounts of 1549. Swift is honoured as the 'Father' of the feoffees and his arms appear in the greave's chain of office.

The feoffees were placed on a more regular basis by a royal charter of 1584. The Queen granted large estates, mostly 'concealed estates' that had been seized by the Crown, in various counties to Laurence Woodnett of Lincoln's Inn and Anthony Collins of London, who on 1 September 1584 transferred estates in Rotherham, Masbrough, Brinsworth and Denaby to William West, gent., of Rotherham, and others, in trust 'to such uses, intents and

Robert Sanderson, Bishop of Lincoln and former pupil of Rotherham Grammar School. The inscription is incorrect as he died in 1663. He would have been 76 in that year. (*Rotherham Central Library*)

purposes as should be agreed upon by the chiefest part of the inhabitants of the said town of Rotherham'. William West was one of the foremost lawyers of his day and was the author of *Symbolographia*, an early legal textbook. He was seneschal to the Earl of Shrewsbury and responsible for running the manor courts in Sheffield and Rotherham. It seems likely that it was West who was responsible for the negotiations that led to the land being sold to Rotherham for £61 5s.

On 3 August 1589 West, Blythe, Burrowes and Browne conveyed the property to the first full body of 12 feoffees, to be held in trust to be employed for the relief of the poor, the maintenance and repair of bridges in and about the town and the discharge of taxes and other common charges. Whenever the body of feoffees was reduced to six by death or removal from Rotherham, another 12 should be elected by the 'chefest and most substanciall part of thinhabitantes of the said towne'. Each year two of the feoffees were to be chosen as 'common greaves' to receive the income from the properties. For many years the greaves' accounts consisted only of a summary of their receipts and expenditure. Guest, however, was able to print a surviving account of Robert Swift and William Whitmore for 1549. These give an idea of the wide area of responsibility of the greaves and feoffees. There are frequent sums for relief of the poor:

to pore pepill on the day of our entre . . . 3s 3d.
to the constables for careying 6 pore men and wemen with 2 litill cartes and 3 horses to Thriber (Thrybergh) . . . 8d.
to Thomas Barowe and his wife when they lay sick . . . 12d.

Other accounts relate to the making or mending of 'yates' or gates on the roads around the town, including gates at the Moor, Eastwood Side, Canklow Field, the Crofts, Badsley Moor Lane and St Ann's Well. They also paid the pinder and for mending the pinfold gate. Payments to the town constables occur frequently, including 12d for mending the constable's axe. Other Tudor accounts show the feoffees' responsibility for the town's archery butts in St Anne's Field and the cleaning and maintenance of the various town wells, the chief of these being the Wellgate wells. In 1553 the accounts contain an early reference to Templeborough, when Robert Machon was paid 2s for six loads of stone from 'Tempyll brouge'. In 1574 they paid for the repair of the pillory (probably in the market-place) and Roger Woodhouse was paid for repairing the 'gybcrake' or gibbet in 1579. Support was also given to the town waits. This body of entertainers were particularly well clothed, for at their first appearance in the accounts in 1579 Roland Robynson was paid 19s 9d for cloth for the waits. In 1593 a total of £2 1s 7d was spent on cloth including 4¾ yd red cloth, 9 yd cotton, 4 'nails' of taffeta, 14 yd of lacings, six dozen buttons, three skeins of thread and unspecified canvas.

In January 1568 the feoffees' accounts contain reference to a reluctant royal visitor to the town, when Mary, Queen of Scots, was moved from Bolton Castle (WRY) to Tutbury Castle (Sts) via Rotherham. Sir Thomas Knollys's account of the journey reads: 'from Pomfrett (Pontefract) to Rotherham 16 myles – and there to lye in the Towne which will also receave the trayne'. The feoffees' accounts contain payments to Mr Lete and Master Bayley for watching the 'Quene of Skottes'. There is unlikely to be any truth in the tradition that she was lodged in the Chapel on the Bridge, which was derelict and wholly unfitted to lodge a royal prisoner. It is more likely that she was lodged in one of the large houses in the town, possibly the Mounteneys' house at the

The Mounteney family house at the bottom of the High Street. It was probably in this house or in an earlier house on this site that Mary, Queen of Scots spent the night in 1568. (*Rotherham Central Library*)

bottom of the High Street. Guest suggests that her train may have found lodging in the Crown at the top of the High Street. From Rotherham she was taken to Godfrey Foljiambe's house near Chesterfield (Dby), then to the Earl of Shrewsbury's manor at Wingfield (Dby), thence to Tutbury. The queen was later moved to Sheffield Castle under the care of the Earl of Shrewsbury, where she was to remain until 1584.

In 1570 the Queen of Scots wrote from Sheffield that the earl was taking her to Chatsworth (Dby) as 'the pestilence was in Rotherham and in other places'. There are references in the feoffees' accounts to outbreaks of the plague in the town, when it was the custom to remove the sick to huts on Rotherham Moor. Money was spent in 1569 on meat and other food to be carried to the moor for the sick families and for warding the moor for five weeks. The extra expenses necessary in 'the plague tyme' were made up by loans from various townspeople. These were paid off in 1592–4 as finances allowed.

The Chapel on the Bridge had to be maintained, as it was an integral part of the bridge. In about 1569 a practical use was found by converting the Chapel into almshouses. We do not know how many unfortunates were accommodated there, but in 1593 6*d* was spent on the poor in the almshouse 'as they lay sicke', and they were given a further 16*d* at Christmas. The feoffees continued to take care of the grammar school, spending money on 'mossinge and ridgeing' the schoolhouse in 1595.

Another structure cared for by the feoffees was the Hood Cross, at the bottom of the High Street at the junction with Doncaster Gate and College Street, which they seem to have been responsible for building. Their 1595 accounts contain sums for 'leading stone to ye Crosse' and Edward Redwarde and the masons were paid 18*d* for 'setting up of ye Crosse' with a further 3*s* 8*d* paid to John Pits for paving. Further money was spent on 72 yd paving at the Hood Cross in 1606 and in 1616 there is reference to the brook by the Hood Cross. Later in the 17th century there are payments to the beadle for 'dressing' the Hood Cross. It is possible that the cross was a watering place on the brook, for in 1630 there is reference to making a new spout at the Hood Cross. There was also a market cross in the market-place, and an 18th-century picture of the market-place shows a cross, surrounded by octagonal steps, and the stocks in front of the medieval town hall. There is reference in 1610 to money paid to the constables for making the town stocks at the market cross.

The manor of Rotherham passed through the hands of various Earls of Shrewsbury during the 16th century but the manor was not always in the hands of the earl himself. In 1592 Rotherham formed part of the jointure or dower of Ann Talbot and brought her a considerable income. Rather than have the trouble of administering the estate herself she had agreed that the

The Rotherham area in the late Tudor period, from Christopher Saxton's map of the West Riding, *c.* 1575. (*Rotherham Central*

earl could hold the estate, paying her an income. This income included £240 for the pastures called the Holmes at Kimberworth, two mills, fair and market tolls from Rotherham with the court perquisites and the tithes of Glossop (Dby), £6 13s 4d for the College House at Rotherham, the £100 that the earl's father paid her above the rent of the parsonage and mill and the rent from all the tenants. Ann Talbot was Ann Herbert, daughter of William, Earl of Pembroke, wife of Francis Talbot, eldest son of George, Earl of Shrewsbury. Francis died in 1582 and, on the death of his father in 1590, the title had passed to Francis' brother Gilbert (d. 1616).

Rotherham started the 16th century on a high with a fine new college and a new parish church packed with finery, the envy of all its neighbours. By the end of the century the town's reputation seems to have fallen somewhat. Hunter prints the Latin lines of a poem, *Iter boreale*, about the town that was circulating in the late 16th century, believing that an English translation would be 'too gross' for his readers. John Guest, believing his readers were made of sterner stuff, provided a translation:

Rotherham, in the County of York, is the first to receive us;
This town was free for gamesters only;
Both host and hostess are excellent gamesters.

Rotherham, which before time was free from gamblers
Now swarms with them;
Denying a sojourn to whomsoever does not know how to gamble.
Although we were indignant at being kept out
Yet we happened to find a better and more honourable place of sojourn.
Now and then that which seems injurious to us is pleasant.

As early as 1551 the manor court had imposed fines for keeping 'unlawfull gammers' in the house and for gaming. It is difficult to imagine any of the abbots of Rufford allowing such a state of affairs to arise during their government of the town.

6

Bell Pits and Slitting Mills

Early Industry

The development of industry in the Don Valley in the area of Rotherham was made inevitable by the geology of the area. The South Yorkshire coal seams dip downwards to the east and a number come to the surface in a circle around Rotherham. Mixed in with these coal seams are bands of iron ore.

The first certain evidence of Roman ironworking in the area was discovered during the excavation at Templeborough in 1916–17. Thomas May uncovered the remains of an industrial complex outside the south-east angle of the fort with a number of clay and stone-lined cavities reddened by heat. These appear to have been used for smelting iron and for glass-making as fragments of both were scattered over the area. There was also a building identified as a smithy with water tanks for quenching forged iron. Analysis of the slag from the smithy suggested that it resulted from the smelting of iron ore similar to that mined at Scunthorpe (Lin). Other finds included a number of crucibles used for melting silver or bronze. The local clays were also exploited and May found a number of examples of pottery made by local potters in imitation of more sophisticated Roman wares. The mineral wealth of the Don Valley area was obviously well known to the Romans, and an important iron-working site has recently been identified at Denaby.

Small-scale exploitation of the local iron ore probably continued during the Dark Ages. We are on more certain ground in the 12th century with the establishment of an industrial complex at Thundercliffe, Kimberworth, where shallow seams of coal were mixed with seams of iron ore. A stream that runs south-south-west from Thorpe Common forms the ancient boundary between the parishes and manors of Ecclesfield, held by Walter de Lovetot, and Kimberworth, held by Richard de Busli. The two lords were approached by the Cistercian monks of Kirkstead Abbey (Lin) who wished to exploit the mineral resources of the area. De Busli's charter is dated to 1161 so it is safe to assume that the Lovetot grant would have been the same year.

Richard de Lovetot granted the monks the site of the Hermitage of St John with land lying between the lands of Richard de Busli (Kimberworth) and of Jordan de Reineville (lord of the sub-manor of Cowley) with all the land that had been held by Robert le Cras (the hermit?) and a further 30 acres. There are two versions of the grant in the Kirkstead Abbey cartulary. The first describes the land in the grant as lying between two streams which T. Walter Hall has identified as the Kimberworth/Ecclesfield boundary stream on the east and another, nameless stream that runs from Jumble Hole Plantation, on the west. To the south the grant extended to Blackburn Brook. The charter also includes the right to pasture 30 beasts in the lands held by de Reineville. The second grant omits the description of the

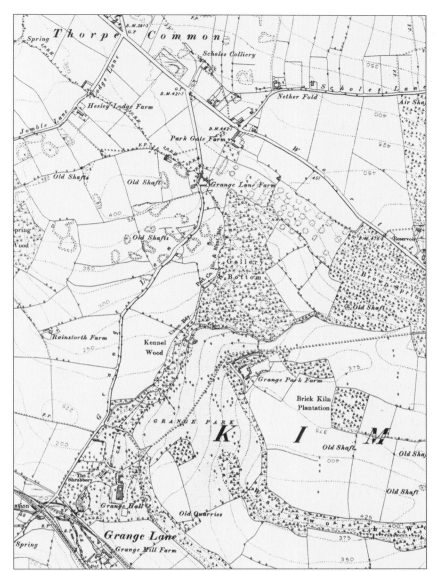

The Thundercliffe area as shown on the Ordnance Survey 6 inch to 1 mile map of 1890. The boundary stream between Kimberworth and Ecclesfield runs through the woods to the east of Grange Lane. Kirkstead Abbey Grange is shown on this map as Park Gate Farm and the remains of bell pits can be seen to the east of Grange Lane Farm. The original Thundercliffe Grange lay on the Kimberworth side of the stream, a short distance to the north-west of its successor, marked as Grange Hall.

bounds and the pasturage rights. William de Lovetot confirmed his father's grant *c*. 1171–81 and in the early 13th century Gerald, son of Gerard de Furnival, William's son-in-law, further confirmed it. Gerard and his wife Matilda (William's daughter and heir), also gave Kirkstead Abbey an acre of land beside the Blackburn Brook to build a mill. Following Gerard's death in the Holy Land in 1218, Matilda confirmed the grant to Kirkstead and gave them the right of free carriage of lead, iron, timber and leather throughout her lands.

Richard de Busli's charter granted the monks a site in Kimberworth for their houses, the right to erect four furnaces, two for smelting iron and two for forging, the right to dig throughout Kimberworth for ore sufficient for the two furnaces and a similar right to collect deadwood to fuel the furnaces. They also had the right to pasture ten oxen and four horses in the common pastures of Kimberworth. There was to be an annual rent of 5*s* which was waived for the first five years. It would seem that initially the ironworks was an experiment, with the right to abandon it after the initial five-year period. The Busli charter did not grant Kirkstead any fixed area of land. The abbey had the right to erect its buildings wherever was found to be most convenient.

Lay brothers would have carried out the actual work of mining, smelting and forging the iron with an overseer from the abbey. The iron ore was either dug from surface outcrops or from shallow shafts known as bell pits. The ore would be dug from around the base of the shaft and wound to the surface in baskets. When the workings had extended far enough to threaten roof falls the pit would be abandoned and a new shaft dug a short distance away. The spoil thrown up around the mouth of the shaft resulted in the characteristic doughnut-shaped earthworks. Once the shallow seams of ore had been worked out, more sophisticated mining methods had to be developed with deeper shafts and adits with the roof supported on timbers. The remains of bell pits can be seen on Thorpe Common, in Grange Park and in Smithy Wood.

The ore was smelted in primitive furnaces known as 'boles', shallow bowl-shaped excavations in the earth surrounded by low stone walls, oriented to catch the prevailing wind. Coal could not be used as fuel because the sulphur content rendered the iron brittle. It was for this reason the de Buslis had given the monks the right to gather deadwood throughout the manor. Converting the timber into charcoal allowed a higher temperature to be attained. A brisk wind raised the internal temperature sufficiently to drive the iron out of the ore but not to melt it completely. Once the melt was complete a spongy mass of iron mixed with slag and impurities was left in the bottom of the hearth. This bloom was then re-heated in the bloomery furnace and subjected to repeated hammering to drive out slag and impurities. The end product was ductile wrought iron that could be converted into tools or weapons by further reheating, hammering and welding. A bole furnace could retrieve about 12.5 per cent of the iron in the ore, and it took around 660 lb of fuel to produce a bloom of about 130–150 lb.

The medieval buildings at Kirkstead Abbey Grange, during restoration in 1900. (*Rotherham Central Library*)

No details survive of the working of the ironworks at Thundercliffe but records do survive of similar works established by the Bishop of Durham at Byrkeknott in Weardale, using 'blomers and colliers' from Rotherham and Wakefield. It is possible, therefore, that the 'smythman or blomer', John Gylle, had received his training at Thundercliffe. The bloom hearth and 'string hearth' took six days to build, at a cost of 3s 4d in labour. From the initial supply of 156 tons of ore Gylle was able to produce 278 blooms, totalling 25 tons. It took six packhorse loads of charcoal to produce one bloom of c. 200 lb. The 'string hearth' was used to refine the bloom. The refined bloom was cut up into workable pieces of c. 16 lb with an axe. The ironmonger who is listed in Rotherham in 1379 was probably engaged in selling such ingots to local blacksmiths and cutlers.

In his recent re-evaluation of the documentary and physical evidence, Mel Jones has suggested that Kirkstead Abbey Grange, on Wortley Road, marks the site of Kirkstead's first area of activity. The buildings lie close to the outcrops of the iron seams and the position on the crest of the valley edge, exposed to the prevailing winds, would have been perfect for the furnaces. They also lay next to the ancient packhorse route from Lancashire and Cheshire to Rotherham and the adjacent common would have been convenient for grazing animals. The present buildings were heavily restored in 1900 and again in 1984–5. Some medieval features remain, however, including a round-headed window that could be 12th-century. The roof timbers have obviously been reused. Mel Jones has suggested that the first buildings were entirely or partly timber-framed and that the present structure is a late medieval rebuilding incorporating earlier material.

In 1984 the Rotherham Archaeological Society began excavating on the site of the original Thundercliffe Grange, built on the site of the medieval works. The house was demolished in the 18th century when the Earl of Effingham built the present Thundercliffe Grange a short distance to the east. The original house stood within the area of the de Lovetot grant in Ecclesfield, on the site of a much earlier forge. Large quantities of medieval and 16th-century pottery were found, including some from the 12th century, along with iron slag and fragments of grindstones. These remains may be the result of a move of operations downhill to take advantage of waterpower. There was formerly a fishpond above the house that could have had its origins as a millpond. The application of waterpower to drive larger bellows allowed much higher temperatures to be achieved. It could also be used to power the forge hammers. Writing in 1935 Sir George Sitwell claimed that water blast was in use in Rotherham as early as 1400–10, but does not give his source or say where the works was situated.

In the middle of the 14th century religious houses were forbidden to engage directly in trade or commerce and, if the works were still in production, they must have been leased out. The iron working activity had covered the area with heaps of slag and cinders that gave the area its alternative name of Cindercliff. When the last abbot provided a list of Kirkstead's possessions at the Dissolution, he did not refer to ironworks at Kimberworth but accounted for the 'grange of Senecliffe'. T. Walter Hall was of the opinion that the monks had given up their iron workings and had ceased to pay the rent. Kirkstead Abbey Grange had reverted to the lord of the manor but they had continued to hold the 200 acres in Ecclesfield parish including Thundercliffe Grange. There is reference to the Rokeby family living at Thundercliffe in the reign of Henry VI, presumably under a lease from Kirkstead. Even if the ironworks were no longer in operation in the early 16th century, the iron ore was obviously still seen as an important asset. In 1524 Brian Hastyng of Campsall had a lease from the

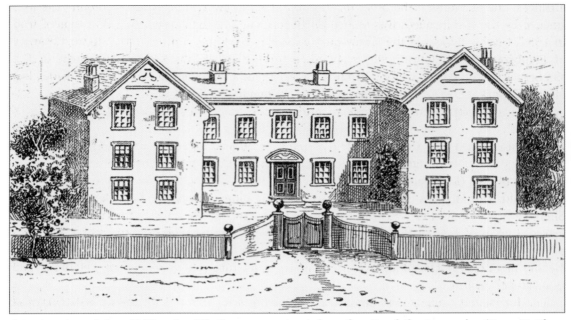

An engraving of the old Thundercliffe Grange, constructed on the site of the ironworks. (*From Matthew, Chapeltown researches, 1893*)

abbot of 'Senocliffe Grange' with the right to dig ironstone in the abbey's lands of Thundercliffe Grange.

Considerable quantities of coal must have been brought to the surface as a by-product of the iron mining. Although this was no use for smelting iron, it was almost certainly used to heat domestic quarters and would have found a ready sale among the local inhabitants. Coal mining was well established when Rotherham was visited by Leland who referred to the very good pits of coal in the area. There are tantalising references to coal mining in other 16th-century documents. The rental of Rufford's Rotherham estates at the Dissolution includes the large half yearly rent of 66s 8d due from Michael Wentworth for the 'Coole pitts'. The Earl of Shrewsbury's Rotherham estate accounts for the Pentecost quarter of 1582 include an entry for £16 10s paid by Ralph Wainwright for 'Kymberworth Coalepyttes'. By the time the Michaelmas 1582 accounts were prepared, Wainwright had sublet the pits to Thomas Spytlehowse and partners. Once the surface outcrops and shallow seams were exhausted, the entrepreneurs began to mine deeper seams by sinking shafts and excavating galleries supported by wooden props.

The invention of the blast furnace, probably in Belgium *c.* 1400, made it possible to extract a far greater proportion of iron from the ore. The first English blast furnaces were built in the Weald in the late 15th century and the technology reached South Yorkshire the following century. The construction of blast furnaces with the associated fineries, chaferies and waterworks required more capital and in the 16th century a number of partnerships arose to exploit the new technology. The topography of the region around Sheffield and Rotherham, well wooded with many swift-flowing streams and available iron ore, lent itself to the establishment of furnaces. The Shrewsbury estate accounts record ironstone mines at Tankersley, a furnace at Wadsley and fineries at Kimberworth in 1578. In 1589 the Earl of Shrewsbury had two blast furnaces, one at Wadsley, the other on the Don at Kimberworth, probably at Jordan. The iron smelted by the two furnaces was refined in the forge at Attercliffe, producing 233 tons of iron in 1587. On the division of the Shrewsbury estates in 1616 the ironworks went to the Countess of Pembroke. Sir William Savile, steward to the Earl of Pembroke, was in charge of the Kimberworth ironworks until his death in 1644. Savile's wife tried to carry on the works, but after two years she was found to have paid no rent and to owe £8,500.

In the mid-17th century the main ironmaster in South Yorkshire was Lionel Copley of Wadworth. As early as 1603 the Copleys were leasing Attercliffe Forge from the Earl of Shrewsbury. In 1638 Copley with two partners was granted permission to build an ironworks at Conisbrough and in 1639 Copley with his brother Christopher, Thomas St Nicholas of Ash (Ken), and Leonard Pinkney of London agreed to lease land at World's End, Ecclesfield, the Holmes, Kimberworth, Castle Meadow, Attercliffe and Dewhurst Close, Sheffield from the Earl of Arundel, agreeing to erect two forges on the land. In 1652 Copley leased 3 acres of land at Rockley to build a blast furnace and took over the remaining term of the lease of Chapeltown Furnace and Kimberworth Forge from the Royalist Francis Neville of Chevet, formerly agent for the South Yorkshire estates of Earl of Pembroke and Countess of Arundel.

The furnace at Chapeltown, capable of producing 450 tons of iron a year, with forges at Attercliffe, Wadsley and Kimberworth, became known as the Duke of Norfolk's ironworks. When he first leased the works Copley was paying £2,000 a year in rent. In the period immediately after the Civil War the works were obviously languishing. When the Committee for Compounding with Delinquents examined Leonard Pinkney in 1646, he claimed to be impoverished, as 'by reason of these troubles the works pays not the rent reserved and the arrears are worth more than the term and the same is subject to a re-entry for nonpayment'. Business must have improved after the Restoration. In December 1666 Copley entered into an agreement with Henry Howard, second son of the late Henry, Earl of Arundel and Surrey, to lease Chapeltown Furnace, Rotherham Forge, Wardsend Forge and Attercliffe Forge for ten years from 3 June 1667 at £200 per year, converting Rotherham Forge into a slitting mill at his own expense. Copley was to have the right to get ironstone from anywhere within the parishes of Ecclesfield and Sheffield where the mineral rights were owned by Howard or by Thomas, Earl of Norfolk (Howard's elder brother). A further clause allowed Copley to take 1,500 cords of wood a year for making charcoal, from the parishes of Sheffield, Ecclesfield, Rotherham, Handsworth, Whiston and Treeton. Each cord was to measure 4 ft × 4 ft × 8 ft, a total of over 5,000 cu. m. of timber each year.

Lionel Copley was the younger son of William Copley of Wadworth. In 1639 he was living at Broom in the parish of Whiston but in 1658 he inherited Wadworth Hall from his nephew. Despite his Parliamentary sympathies, Copley managed to keep hold of his enterprises at the Restoration. He based his operations in Rotherham where he occupied the largest house in the town, assessed at 19 hearths in 1665. He also rented coalmines at Kimberworth and Whiston, paying rents of £100 and £55 respectively. He appears to have made a few enemies in Rotherham. In 1644 an indictment was found against him at York for beating Richard Firth at Rotherham, putting a bridle in his mouth, and riding him round the town, kicking him to make him move. In August 1666 Samuel and Ruth Wood were fined 13s 4d each and placed in the pillory at Rotherham for conspiring to defraud Copley. The following year Francis Mounteney of Rotherham was convicted of inciting the Woods to make charges against Copley. Lionel Copley died in London in December 1675 and was buried at Wadworth.

Much of the iron produced at Chapeltown furnace and refined at Attercliffe would have been sent to the new slitting mill at Masbrough to be cut into rods for the local nailing industry. The power for the mills and furnaces here came from the river Don, flowing through the Holmes Goit. The rods were bought by nail chapmen, middlemen who supplied the nailers in the surrounding villages. Nailing was a seasonal occupation, when agricultural work was slack. Considerable quantities of rod were slit at Masbrough in the late 17th and early 18th centuries, taking iron from both Wortley and Attercliffe forges. In 1691 Masbrough slit 104 tons of rod, rising to 152 tons in 1704. The 1730s saw the nail trade hit by competition from nails made in Worcestershire and Staffordshire where labour was cheaper but trade must have picked up in the 1740s for in 1744 Masbrough slit a total of 309 tons. Demand was so high that a new slitting mill with an annual capacity of c. 200 tons was erected at Attercliffe in 1747–8. Much of the output was sold to the nail factors in Sheffield, but after 1744 the biggest customer for the Masbrough rod was the London concern of William Sitwell and Co. who supplied nailers in Rotherham, Ecclesfield and Eckington (Dby). Between 1744 and 1755 they bought over £14,000-worth of rod from Masbrough. The outbreak of the Seven Years War in 1756 caused a severe slump in trade, but even so Joseph Hague, who had been employed making nails in Rotherham by the Fell partnership, bought £7,000-worth of rod from Masbrough during the war.

The reference to timber in Copley's agreement is a reminder of the insatiable appetite of the early ironworks for charcoal. South Yorkshire was well wooded in Tudor times and much of the timber for charcoal was cut from managed woodland. Despite this, by the early 18th century clear felling without replacement and the clearance of woodland for farming caused a shortage of timber that was a serious limitation on the South Yorkshire ironworks. The rich woodland of the Rivelin valley disappeared into the Copley ironworks and was not replanted, leaving the valley waste for some years. Other timber resources were more responsibly managed. A document of c. 1600 lists spring or coppice woods on the Shrewsbury estate in South Yorkshire, including Treeton Wood, Canklow Wood, Wickersley Wood, Bassingthorpe Spring, Walkworth Wood and 300 acres of timber in Kimberworth Park. The Wentworth Woodhouse estate contained over 1,000 acres of woodland, the largest single wood being Tinsley Wood. In 1657 Lionel Copley agreed with the Earl of Strafford for the felling of underwood and trees in 13 woods on the Wentworth estate, including Tinsley Park (396 acres) and other woods at Brampton Bierlow, Elsecar and Wentworth.

Steel (iron with a carbon content of between 0.25 per cent and 1.7 per cent) was made in small quantities from early times by heating wrought iron in charcoal so that the iron absorbed carbon. The quality of the steel depended entirely on the skill of the smith in judging the temperature of the forge. Larger quantities could be made in the cementation furnace introduced from the Continent in the early 17th century. This process involved packing iron bars in charcoal inside a fireclay chest and heating the chest in a reverberatory furnace to convert the iron into 'blister steel', so called because of the appearance of the finished bars. Because the iron was not subject to direct heat, coal could be used to fire the furnace.

It was probably for some form of cementation furnace for which Charles Tooker of Moorgate Hall obtained a patent in 1666 with the assistance of Sir John Reresby of Thrybergh, against the objections of the Cutlers Company of Hallamshire who obtained its reversal the same year. Tooker's furnace may have been near his house in Moorgate, for in

1692 John Tooker, his son, took a new lease from the feoffees at a rent of 10s a year of a messuage, foldstead, two furnaces and a smithy in Moorgate for which Charles had previously paid £3 per year. Some of the buildings had been pulled down and there was a general depression of property values in the area. The Tookers also had an interest in a steel works on the Don at Thrybergh. In 1664 Charles took a lease from Sir John Reresby of 'all the water course which was lately used for a steel mill or forge called Thriburgh Steele Forge', formerly leased by Charles's father, also Charles Tooker. The lease included an existing mill but contained a proviso that Reresby's corn mill was to have priority of water in times of scarcity and that the fulling mill at Thrybergh was to have priority when there was cloth in the stocks. The rent was £10 10s a year for a 21-year term. Three years later Tooker sold a quarter share in the steel forge to Robert Harrison of Richmond and Robert Harrison the younger of Handsworth Woodhouse. The Harrisons are known to have operated a steel furnace at Richmond, Handsworth, in the late 17th century.

In the late 17th and early 18th centuries the ironworks in South Yorkshire were part of a series of shifting, interconnected partnerships of which the Fell, Simpson and Spencer families were prominent. On Lionel Copley's death in 1675 William Simpson, an attorney who allegedly used his position as executor to cheat Copley's son out of his inheritance, acquired his ironworking interests. The Fell partnership also dealt in steel, some of which was obtained from a furnace in Rotherham. In 1709 the partnership's representative, Field Sylvester, paid Dysney Staniforth £37 12s 6d for 'all that steele furnace with smithy and tenting belonging thereto situate in Rotherham in or near the beast market' (i.e. near the Crofts). This furnace must have been close to the site of Tooker's earlier enterprise. In the following year Sylvester was accounting for £10 11s 3d for 'Mr. Stanyford's Furnace at Rotherham'. This furnace was out of use by 1717 by which time a barn had been built on the site. By the early 18th century shortage of timber for charcoal was having a serious effect on the South Yorkshire ironworks. In 1724 the partners in the Duke of Norfolk's ironworks were buying timber from as far away as Thurnscoe and Darfield. When the Fell partnership took a new lease of the Duke of Norfolk's ironworks in 1727, the number of cords of wood they were allowed annually from the local woods had fallen to 800. At this time the total assets of the partnership were valued at £15,000. The Fell partnership, however, failed to adapt to new technology introduced in the 18th century. By the middle of the century their star was falling and a new star, the Walkers of Masbrough, was in the ascendant. The Walkers were ready to embrace new technology and to seize the opportunities that arose through the improvements brought to road transport by the turnpike trusts and the arrival in Rotherham of the Don Navigation.

7

Civil War and Dissent

The Seventeenth Century

The early years of the 17th century saw the inhabitants of Rotherham and Kimberworth adjusting to yet another change in the lordship of the manors. The direct line of the family of Talbot, Earls of Shrewsbury, failed in 1617 when the 7th and 8th Earls died within a year without male issue. The title passed to a distant branch of the family. The three daughters of the 7th Earl inherited the bulk of the Sheffield, Rotherham and other estates.

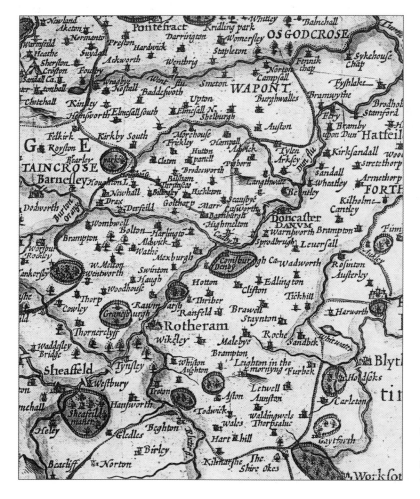

John Speed's map of the West Riding (1610) shows only towns, villages, rivers and parks. (*Rotherham Central Library*)

All three had married into the aristocracy. The eldest daughter, Mary, had married William Herbert, Earl of Pembroke, in 1604. The second sister, Elizabeth, married Henry Grey, Earl of Kent, while the youngest, Alethea, married Thomas Howard, Earl of Arundel and Surrey. In 1627, when it became clear that neither of the elder sisters would produce an heir, the three earls and their wives entered into a settlement. The manors of Sheffield, Colley, Kimberworth, Wadsley, Worrall, Whiston, Treeton, Rotherham and Dinnington, with the rectories of Sheffield, Tickhill and Rotherham, and various other estates in Yorkshire and Nottinghamshire, were conveyed in trust for the Earl of Pembroke and his wife for their lives, with remainder to Henry Howard, Lord Maltravers, for his life and remainder to Thomas Howard and the heirs of his body. Thomas Howard, Earl of Arundel, was granted the additional title of Earl of Norfolk in 1644 but died in exile in Italy in 1646. His wife died in exile in Amsterdam in 1654. The Howard titles descended to her grandson Thomas, to whom the title of Duke of Norfolk was restored by Charles II in 1660. The management of the South Yorkshire estates was entrusted to his brother Henry Howard, who inherited the dukedom and the estates when Thomas died, unmarried, in 1677.

In the 1660s and 1670s we find Henry Howard, on his brother's behalf, defending his right to force all tenants to use the manorial corn mills. In 1663 Ellen Dickenson, widow, and Thomas Owen, her tenant, were prosecuted for bypassing the lord's mills by grinding corn on a horse-powered mill, erected by Ellen's husband. Their claim of ignorance of the custom was rejected and the verdict was used as a precedent in 1672 in a similar case against Joseph Drew, Ralph Woollen, Thomas Greenwood and John Eaton. After three trials in 1676 the verdict was given that Drew, Greenwood and Eaton were tenants of the manor, owing suit of mill, but that Woollen and other free tenants owed no such suit. If, however, their grain was unground after 48 hours, they had the right to remove it to another mill. It was Henry, 5th Duke of Norfolk, who severed Rotherham and Kimberworth from the Hallamshire estates. On the death of his first wife, Lady Ann Somerset, he married Jane Bickerton and impoverished the family by his bequests to her. These included the Rotherham and Kimberworth estates. After his death in 1684 Jane became the lady of the manor, and established her household at the Holmes, Masbrough. On her death in 1693 her bowels were buried in the chancel of Rotherham parish church, while the remainder of her body was buried elsewhere, probably at the Howard family seat of Arundel (Ssx). Rotherham and Kimberworth passed to her eldest son, George Howard.

The manor court continued to regulate the life of the town, much of its business being taken up with the open fields and their cultivation. In a number of the open fields it had been the custom to allow portions to be enclosed provided the closes were laid fallow with the remainder of the field at Michaelmas. In 1572, for example, Francis Talbot, then lord of the manor, allowed Mistress Whitmore to make and sow Wheat Close within Cross Field, Eastwood, for one year and no longer, provided it was thrown fallow with the remainder of the field. The common was stinted, in other words the number of beasts that could be pastured was limited and shared among those with common rights. Each cottager was allowed to pasture two 'beasts' (cattle) or two horses (or one of each). Farmers who had a plough could pasture as many oxen as they needed for the plough. Every inhabitant with land in the open fields was allowed to pasture six sheep on the Common from May Day (1 May) until Lammas (1 August) for every acre of arable that they held. Sheep had to be herded under the highway across the Moor towards Whiston, known as the 'hye gate or london way'. Any sheep that strayed above the highway could be impounded by the

The Turf Tavern (formerly the Boot and Shoe) on Bridgegate is one of Rotherham's lost timber-framed buildings, having been demolished when Bridgegate was widened in 1928. The surface 'half-timbering' on the first floor is false, having been added by Bentley's Brewery in the late 19th century. (*Rotherham Central Library*)

byerlawmen or the pinder and kept until the owner paid for their release at the rate of 4*d* per score. On the day after Michaelmas (30 September) the byerlawmen, constables, pinder and some of the inhabitants went around the open fields throwing open any enclosures that had been made. This seems to have become the occasion for annual celebrations. In 1624 19*s* 4*d* was spent on two cheeses, five dozen of bread and 12 or 13 gallons of ale 'bestowed of the Byerlaw men' at their meeting at Gallowtree Hill (on Clifton Lane) at their meeting to cast open the closes.

It is in 1617 that there is first reference to payment by the feoffees of 'chiminage' to the lord of the manor of Whiston for the use of a road from the Mile Oaks to the top of Rotherham Moor. This was the direct route from the West Riding to the south and would have been heavily used by carriers and packhorse trains. Previously the Earl of Shrewsbury had charged a toll for passage from the Mile Oaks to Canklow Lydgate. The original road ran from the Hood Cross up Wellgate and then diagonally across Broom Valley to the Mile Oak (where the present Mile Oak Road joins Moorgate). This route bypassed the market-place and in 1617 was changed to a more direct route across the Moor and through the Beast Market to the top of the High Street 'for the general good of the towne and specially the Inkepers in the hyestrete and tradesmen in the Market-stede'. The cost of the 'chiminage' was £1 6*s* 8*d*, which continued to be paid until the road was turnpiked in the mid-18th century. In 1630 the new route was described as running the direct way from the Mile Oaks to Arthur Burnley's house near Moorgate Hall. An avenue of 52 oak trees originally lined the road from there into Rotherham until Burnley cut them down to build his house in the 1620s.

John Ogilby's road map of 1675 shows the London–Richmond (NRY) road passing through Aughton and Whiston and crossing Rotherham Moor into the town across Rotherham Bridge and via Greasbrough to Barnsley. Another important route into Rotherham was the ancient salt way from the Cheshire salt mines. Salt was necessary for preserving food in the pre-refrigeration age and large quantities were required. The packhorse trains carrying the salt from Cheshire crossed the Pennines via Woodhead Pass, passing into Yorkshire at Saltersbrook and travelling via Wortley, Chapeltown and Kimberworth, down Psalters Lane into Rotherham. Salt was not the only commodity carried on the route. Cheese, potatoes and manufactured goods were brought from Manchester while hemp, flax and German yarn were carried in the opposite direction. The other main routes out of the town were via Westgate via Tinsley to Sheffield and eastwards via Thrybergh to Doncaster. Wellgate also gave access to the road to Bawtry, then an important river port.

The feoffees' accounts continue to show their concern for the upkeep of Rotherham Bridge and the Bridge Chapel. In 1624 the considerable sum of £16 14s was spent on repair of half of Rotherham Bridge, 'our part of the bridge being much decayed'. A further £15 19s 11d was spent on clothing the poor and repairing the almshouse (i.e. the Bridge Chapel) 'for certain poor lame and aged'. The Hood Cross was in frequent need of repair with regular entries for stone, timber and labour for its upkeep. The wooden pinfold, which stood in Pinfold Lane, off Wellgate, was rebuilt in stone in 1643. The town stocks near the market cross were rebuilt in 1610, the town's tankard (presumably used at feasts) was repaired in 1636, and the town drum was mended in 1610 and 1637. A bellman or watchman was employed to patrol the town at night. When in 1620 the Earl's agent took it upon himself to appoint the bellman, the feoffees were quick to assert their rights.

The manorial bakehouse against the churchyard wall was damaged by fire at least twice during the 17th century. The remains of the bakehouse, including the base of the oven, seen here, were uncovered during the construction of All Saints Square in 1930. (*Rotherham Central Library*)

The old building of the Grammar School in Jesus Gate was also a frequent cause of expense. 1636 saw the expenditure of 15s 2d on repairs to damage to the schoolhouse caused when the common bakehouse caught fire. (The foundations of the bakehouse, which stood behind the schoolhouse, against the churchyard wall were discovered in 1930 when All Saints' Square was being constructed.) It burned down again in 1673, destroying part of the schoolhouse. Two dictionaries were bought at York for the school in 1621 and bound in calfskin. A further dictionary was purchased in 1629. The feoffees seem to have had trouble keeping masters in the early 17th century. Thomas Barrow, however, stayed for 13 years and sent a steady stream of pupils from the grammar school to Oxford or Cambridge. When he moved to Chesterfield Grammar School in 1634 James Wrayte was appointed, but died shortly afterwards. The feoffees then offered the post to Charles Hoole.

Hoole was born in Sheffield in 1609, the son of a shoemaker. The family moved to Wakefield and Charles was educated at Wakefield Grammar School and Lincoln College, Oxford. He was related to Robert Sanderson and seems to have owed his advancement at Rotherham to another relative, Edward Gill of Car House. Hoole found that the boys at Rotherham were taught to construe Greek and Latin well but were 'barren of proper words and good phrases for speaking or writing'. Less able pupils were not making much progress and he was forced to alter the system and introduce new books. Rather than teach all ages

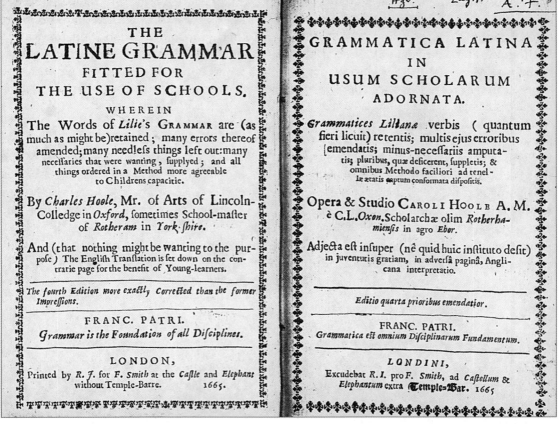

The title pages, in English and Latin, from *The Latine grammar fitted for the use of schools* by Charles Hoole, 'sometimes School-master of Rotheram'. (*Rotherham Central Library*)

and abilities together, he divided the school into separate classes, with the older pupils helping the younger. The school day began at 7 a.m., winter and summer. Morning school finished at 11 a.m. The finish of afternoon school varied. It was 5 p.m. on Monday, Wednesday and Friday, at 4 p.m. on Tuesday and at 3 p.m. on Thursday. Hoole left Rotherham in 1637, and it was not until 1660 that his treatise on education was published, *A new discovery of the old art of teaching schoole in four small treatises*. The title pages states that it had been 'written about Twenty three yeares ago, for the benefit of Rotherham School, where it was first used; and after 14 years trial by diligent practise in London, in many particulars enlarged'. This was the first of a string of school text-books that Hoole was to publish before his death in 1667.

The accounts of the town constables for the early 17th century, throwing a little light on crime of the period, are printed by Guest. In 1608 they accounted for their expenses in apprehending Brian Mounser for the murder of Richard Relfe, taking him before Lord Darcy, watching the corpse until the coroner could view it and transporting Mounser to jail at York. In 1610 Ralf and Thomas Birkey of Preston in Amounderness were apprehended for stealing a purse from Thomas Burley of Whiston, William Raubye accused of stealing a spoon from Thomas Okes, linen draper, and Robert Richmond, late of Ossett (WRY), taken upon suspicion of receiving purses stolen by Ellen Shaw and Ann Hincliffe. In the second half of the century the Rotherham area suffered from the attentions of the notorious highwayman John Nevison, whose gang was based at the Talbot, Newark (Ntt). When their associate Elizabeth Burton was examined before Sir John Reresby she admitted to knowledge of several robberies carried out by the gang, including £200 taken at Maltby from one Malim of Rotherham on his way to Gainsborough Market and £30 stolen near Rotherham from a butcher on his way to Rotherham Fair. She also admitted that she had gone into hiding in Rotherham after a robbery at Mansfield (Ntt) by two of the gang, who warned her to keep quiet. Nevison was arrested in 1676 for a robbery at York but was reprieved and returned to his old ways. He was arrested again, at Sandal (WRY), in 1684 for a trifling robbery and executed at York.

The responsibility for the maintenance of the fabric and furniture of the church and the parsonage lay with the churchwardens whose early accounts, mixed up with those of the feoffees, were printed by Guest. The accounts for 1566 refer to mending 'one of the bokkes that is cheyned in the church', to red leather for covering the Bibles and service books and for boards and lead replacing on the roof. November 1600 saw large celebrations for some reason unknown. The church bells must have been rung all day, as 26 ringers were paid 10d each. Fourteen gallons of ale were purchased from Richard Edmoundes and Bryan Shaw's wife, and consumed, and the churchwardens, minister, parish clerk and the bellman were entertained to supper. A continuing expense was the maintenance of the church, with the purchase of stone, boards and lime. There are also frequent mentions of maintenance of the church bells and repairs to the church clock. The present pulpit was placed in the church in 1604. Later in the century it was moved into the centre of the church, under the western tower arch. The nave was filled with large 'horse box' pews, erected by individual parishioners. These were placed wherever the owner dictated, but in general the upper classes occupied the front ranks with the middle classes at the rear and the poor at the sides.

When the Scots refused to accept a new prayer book, Charles I recalled his ablest servant Thomas Wentworth of Wentworth Woodhouse, whose family owned property in Rotherham, from Ireland to help enforce his will, creating him Earl of Strafford in January 1640. He advised the king to recall Parliament, which had not met for 11 years. This advice rebounded on Strafford as the Commons refused to vote money for the Scottish War. Parliament accused Strafford of planning to bring over an Irish army to support the king, but he defended himself ably and they were forced to abandon judicial process and pass a bill of attainder against him. The earl was executed on 12 May 1641 and the events that were to lead to the outbreak of war between king and Parliament had been put in train. In April 1642 Hull refused entry to the king. On 22 August 1642 Charles I raised his standard at Nottingham and the Civil War had begun. Two days earlier Prince Rupert had passed through Rotherham on his way from landing at Tynemouth to join his uncle at Nottingham.

The outbreak of the Civil War found the majority of townspeople, as at Sheffield, favouring the side of Parliament against Charles I. Most of the local gentry, such as the Westbys and the Gills, shared this view with a minority, such as the Reresbys of Thrybergh, favouring the Royalist side. Joseph Hunter describes the Vicar of Rotherham, the Rev. John Shaw, as a 'most uncompromising parliamentarian'. A fellow pupil of John Milton at Christ's College, Cambridge, Shaw had been fired by the preaching of Thomas Weld who had been ejected from his living in Essex for refusing to subscribe to High Church 'ceremonies'. Philip, Earl of Pembroke, presented him to the living at Rotherham in 1638, on the death of Shaw's cousin, the Rev. William Dickenson. We owe much of our knowledge of Rotherham during the Civil War to John Shaw, who in 1663–4 wrote his memoirs for his son. Other details are included in the prefaces to the published versions of his sermons.

The first act of the war in South Yorkshire was an attack in August or September 1642 on the house of Sir Edward Rodes at Great Houghton, near Barnsley, by a party of Royalists led by Captain Grey. When news of this reached Rotherham, the inhabitants assembled on Rotherham Moor and began to throw up rudimentary earthworks round the town. In Sheffield the castle was seized by a Parliamentary force from Derbyshire, led by Sir John Gell.

On Sunday 22 January 1643, 'the poore towne of Rotherham having neither walls, bulwarks, garrison, fortification, watch etc.', a force of Royalists from Pontefract and Doncaster attempted to seize Rotherham between 10 and 11 a.m. Shaw, no doubt exaggerating, put their number at 6–700. News of the attack was brought to the vicar and his congregation in the parish church. Some 20 or 25 men seized muskets and 'without order, rank, file or almost any skill' set off the resist the invaders. For an hour and a half a battle raged around the Hood Cross until the Cavaliers were driven up Doncaster Gate and out of the town. Afraid that his Puritan views would make him a target for the Royalists, the vicar hid in the steeple until the attackers had been driven off. As he felt that the country was 'full of turmoil and dangers', Shaw fled to Hull, leaving his children with his mother in Rotherham. At Hull the governor, Sir John Hotham, refused to allow him to stay and Shaw made his way back to Rotherham via Beverley (ERY) and Selby (WRY) where, on 15 February 1643, he preached a sermon to the army of Ferdinando, Lord Fairfax, Parliament's commander in Yorkshire. Shaw returned to Rotherham to find that Fairfax had established a small garrison in the town 'for the safe guarding of these parts of the country from the violent plunderings of unruly soldiers and other disaffected to the King and parliament'. In February 1643 Capt. William Fairfax and Captain Francis Stanley, the commanders of the Rotherham garrison, wrote to the parish constables in the area requiring contributions towards the maintenance of 'scowt horses' at Rotherham. Rawmarsh, Mexborough and Sprotbrough were required to contribute 25s each.

In the spring of 1643 William Cavendish, Earl of Newcastle, the king's commander in the northern counties, decided to clear the Parliamentarians from the south of Yorkshire. He moved on Rotherham with 8,000 men in preparation for an assault on Sheffield Castle. The feoffees' accounts for 1643 include a sum of £10 due to Mr Malym and Thomas Rigg 'towards the money they laid downe for the common Armes'. In May 1643 the Royalists advanced south through Masbrough but when they came to Rotherham Bridge they found it barricaded by the townspeople, aided by a party of 30 boys from the Grammar School who manned the town's only cannon. They caused considerable casualties among the attacking force, among the dead being Capt. Francis Errington of Denton. The town was short of gunpowder as supplies intended for Rotherham had been captured at Gainsborough (Lin), but the defenders managed to keep the royal army at bay for 48 hours. When their ammunition had run out and several houses had been set on fire by enemy grenades, they had to sue for peace. A few days later Lord Fairfax wrote to William Lenthall, Speaker of the House of Commons, to inform him that: 'the Forces in Rotherham held out two dayes siege and yielded up the Town upon Treaty, wherein it was agreed that the Town should not be plundered and that the gentleman Commanders and Soldiers (six only excepted, that were specially named),

William Cavendish, Marquis of New-castle, Gen. of his Majesties Army, in the North.

William Cavendish, Earl, later Marquis (1643) and Duke (1665), of Newcastle, commander of the Royalist army that captured Rotherham in 1643.

leaving their Arms should have free liberty to go wither they pleased. . . .'

However, the terms of surrender were soon forgotten and the town was plundered. The defenders were made prisoner and the Royalists did their best to persuade them to change sides. Sir John Gell, the Parliamentary commander in Derbyshire, intended to give battle at Rotherham to the royal army but had scarcely begun his march when he heard of the town's fall. The garrison at Sheffield Castle, hearing of the fall of Rotherham and the approach of some of Newcastle's forces, abandoned their defences and fled to Chesterfield or Manchester.

The Earl of Newcastle imposed fines of 1,000 marks (£666) on the town and individually on William Spencer of Attercliffe Hall and Bramley Grange, Henry Westby of Car House, George Westby of Guilthwaite (Spencer's brother-in-law and nephew of Henry Westby) and the Rev. John Shaw. The first three were taken prisoner but Shaw managed to evade capture. Shaw later gave varying accounts of his escape. In his autobiography Shaw states that he and his servant, Robert Gee, hid in the steeple of the parish church and 'the soldiers sought me diligently – plundered my house, and came five or six times into the very room where we were'. His sermon, *The three kingdome's case* (London, 1646), tells a different tale. In this he claimed that, having heard of the enemy's 'speciall intent to ruine the minister of the place', he made his way unobserved through the crowds and hid in the vault or attic of an uninhabited house. Unfortunately Cavaliers proceeded to commandeer the house as their guardhouse. The town was thoroughly searched, the searchers even thrusting their sword through the floorboards of the room in which he was hidden. He remained undiscovered for three days and nights (4 to 6 May), with no food or drink, not daring to stir lest he be discovered. On the third night hunger drove him downstairs to find the house uninhabited and he made his way to his own house, not knowing that some Cavaliers were billeted there. Luckily a friend diverted him at the last moment and he got into another house, where he lay on the earthen floor for three weeks before he managed to escape to Manchester.

According to Lord Fairfax, the capture of Rotherham and Sheffield 'much elated the enemy and cast down the spirits of the people of these parts. . . . The Earl of Newcastle's Army do now range over all the Southwest part of the Countrey, pillaging and cruelly using the well affected party'. The Royalists remained in command of South Yorkshire until the defeat of Prince Rupert's army at Marston Moor on 2 July 1644. At the end of 1643 Parliament had entered into an alliance with the Scots and it was 1,200 Scottish foot with a regiment of horse under Major General Crawford who drove the Royalist garrison out of Rotherham in August 1644. Sheffield Castle surrendered to Crawford on 11 August after a short but intense bombardment. Rotherham's foremost Royalist, Major Richard Mounteney, was commander of the garrison at Tickhill which surrendered to Cromwell in July 1644. In August 1645 the Scots army under David Leslie was quartered in Rotherham. The men were in poor condition and could have been cut off by the Royalists at Barnby Moor (Ntt) if they had shown any initiative. The following year saw the defeat of the king's army at Naseby (Nht) by the New Model Army commanded by Sir Thomas Fairfax. When Oxford fell to Parliament in June 1646 Charles I fled to take refuge with the Scots army, then besieging Newark (Ntt). In July Parliament sent a commission, including the Earl of Pembroke, accompanied by the Rev. John Shaw as chaplain, to Newark to offer peace terms to the king. The Scots army withdrew north to Newcastle, taking the king with them. When Charles rejected the hard terms demanded by the Scots, they came to an agreement with Parliament to withdraw from England and to hand over the king to Parliament's commissioners.

Rotherham received a second reluctant royal visitor in February 1647 when Charles I was lodged in the town on his way south as a prisoner of Parliament. It is likely that, like Mary, Queen of Scots, he was lodged in the Mounteneys' house on the south side of the High Street. Some of his household may have stayed at the Elephant and Castle. While the king was in the town the young Sir John Reresby visited him from Thrybergh. Reresby relates in his memoirs that the king told him he 'was the son of an honest man'. One of the means employed by Parliament to defray the cost of the war was to sequester the estates of Royalists and force them to pay a fine of two years' estimated value of the estate plus one tenth of their goods and chattels for their return. Thomas Nelson of Rotherham, vintner, admitted to being in arms against Parliament and was fined £6 13s 4d. Francis Stringer of Whiston, who possessed tithes at Greasbrough, Dalton and Morthen, within the parish of Rotherham, was fined £133. Alethea, Countess of Arundel and Surrey, who had fled to the Netherlands, fought to prevent Parliament selling two thirds of her estate, including the manors of Rotherham and Sheffield. The matter was not settled until after her death in 1654 and her estate was forced to pay the huge fine of £19,000.

Although Rotherham had not taken a major part in the Civil War, the war and its aftermath seem to have had a depressing effect on local trade and the prosperity of the town. On 12 October 1658 the West Riding justices meeting at Doncaster received a petition from the town. This related that:

> the Towne of Rotherham . . . in former times was populous & wealthy & well able to supply the wants and yeilde helpe to the neighbouring townes in times of need, now since of late years that the inhabitants . . . are falne into greate decay . . . & growne numerous in theire poore who are not only become a great burthen to the said Towne encreasing daily upon them . . . if those of the said pore who are able to worke will not be sett to worke and employed in some trade or calling which may in some good measure supply their present necessityes & trayne up theire children from time to time for theire further subsistence, the utter ruyne of the Towne cannot be avoyded. . . .

Luckily the feoffees had been blessed with 'hearts to set themselves to the advancement of soe good a worke' and they had devised a scheme to establish a cloth industry in the town to train the poor to make fustians (coarse cotton or linen cloth) and Manchester ware (cotton goods). The justices agreed to order that any paupers who refused to enter the scheme would forfeit their right to poor relief and become liable to prosecution. Paupers who persisted with begging door to door within the West Riding were to be arrested and prosecuted as vagrants.

The money to finance this employment scheme seems to have come from a legacy of £100 left to the poor of Rotherham by the Earl of Shrewsbury in 1617. The money was used as a source of small loans to local businessmen. The interest was allowed to accrue until £300 had accumulated and thereafter the interest was used to apprentice pauper children and support the aged while the principal continued to accumulate. It was this principal that the feoffees used to lease and fit out a workhouse. It was some time before the scheme showed a profit. In 1659 a total of £229 9s 7d was spent fitting out and reglazing the workhouse and buying materials. The first year's trading resulted in a loss, with £360

This building in the Crofts, latterly the parish workhouse, may have been the cottage purchased by the feoffees in 1659 to house their job creation scheme employing paupers to weave cloth. (*Author*)

1s 10d received from the sale of fustians and yarn and expenses amounting to £384 12s 3d. In 1661 the figures were: income of £208 4s 3d; expenditure of £217 5s 1d. The loss was greater in 1662 with only £37 9s 2d income against £118 1s 8d spent on 'servants wages, and to the children for their work, carryage of Fustians, wooll & yearne, whiteinge of yearne, candles, coal etc.'. In 1663 the project made a small profit of £6 11s 4d. The following year's accounts are more detailed, showing a total of £236 1s 8d from fustians sold in London and 'in the country' and sales of candlewick and cotton wool. A more substantial profit (£40 6s 5d) was made in 1666 but thereafter the workhouse ceases to be mentioned in the accounts, and this interesting experiment must have come to an end. Unfortunately no indication is given of the number of paupers employed in the scheme or the location of the workhouse. It may perhaps have been the same house, in the north-east corner of the Crofts, which was later used by the overseers as a parish workhouse.

The feoffees shared the care of the poor in the town with the overseers of the poor, an office introduced by the Elizabethan poor law legislation of 1597–1601. Overseers were elected by an annual vestry meeting and normally served for one year. In large parishes, such as Rotherham, each township elected its own overseers. The earliest surviving accounts for Rotherham date only from 1672 when Jonathan Staniforth, gent., William Standley, Joseph Sorsby and John Broughton were overseers. Their expenses included a warrant against John Thompson for 'incontinency' with Mary Barwicke and expenses concerning the removals of Edward Hargreaves, Elizabeth Stephenson and Isabell Royston. John Stanyforth had to attend the Quarter Sessions at Barnsley to establish that Elizabeth Stephenson did not have a legal settlement in Rotherham. There are also regular sums for visits to Thrybergh and Worsbrough, to the local justices of the peace, to have warrants sworn and removal orders countersigned.

Rotherham did not, of course, escape from the religious turmoil that beset the country during the century, with the established Anglican Church attempting to stem the growing tide of nonconformity. In 1647 the Rev. Henry Revell of Rotherham, William Crofts of Doncaster, and Robert Brown of Rotherham, were charged with publishing *The parliament's ten commandments*, a blasphemous and seditious pamphlet. This was held to be a profane and wicked parody of the Lord's Prayer, the creed and the ten commandments. Revell was fined £50, the others £100 each. After the Rev. John Shaw escaped from Rotherham in 1643, he made his way via Manchester to Hull where he remained until he returned to Rotherham in June 1662. The Rev. Luke Clayton, 'a Prophet that had unusual honour in his own Country', had been appointed vicar of Rotherham in 1642, following Shaw's flight. For several years Clayton preached twice a day 'to a numerous Congregation' and repeated the substance of his sermon in the evening. He was of a Presbyterian persuasion but was not in favour of complete religious toleration. In 1652 Elizabeth Hooton, a Quaker, came to Rotherham and preached to the congregation as they left church. Clayton had her arrested and imprisoned at York. After Shaw's return to Rotherham, for a few months both he and Shaw preached on Sundays, and sometimes in midweek. On 24 August 1662, however, the Act of Uniformity came into force, requiring all clergy to subscribe to the Thirty-Nine Articles, to use the same form of service and to use only the new 1661 *Book of Common Prayer*. Throughout England over 2,000 clergy, of Puritan or Presbyterian persuasion, found themselves unable to comply with the legislation and were ejected from their livings. Both Clayton and Shaw refused to subscribe and Clayton was accordingly ejected from the vicarage. As no successor was appointed, Clayton continued to hold services in the parish

The building in Allenby's Yard, Church Street, where the Dissenters held their meetings in the late 17th century. These buildings were demolished in 1938. (*Rotherham Central Library*)

church, although he laid himself open to imprisonment by doing so. He finally gave up the living in April 1663 when the Rev. James Rigby was appointed. Both Clayton and Shaw continued to preach in the town and Clayton suffered several terms of imprisonment at York for his beliefs. Shaw remained in Rotherham, preaching to his own family and to others, but was under constant suspicion. In November 1663 Shaw with his wife and children were at the house of his son-in-law Jonathan Staniforth, under surveillance by 'a wicked, loose, young man', Francis Mounteney. Mounteney sent to the magistrate Sir Francis Fane at Aston Hall for a warrant to apprehend Shaw, believing that they were preaching in the house and receiving communion. By the time the warrant arrived the party had dispersed to their own houses. Shaw was nevertheless brought before Fane the next day but nothing could be proved. The Rev. John Shaw died in Rotherham on 17 April 1672, aged 65, and was buried in the parish church. When the Declaration of Indulgence eased the restrictions on nonconformists in 1672, Luke Clayton was able to obtain a licence as a general preacher and preached frequently at the chapel of ease at Greasbrough. An application to license Trinity House at Greasbrough, owned by the Earl of Strafford, as a Presbyterian meeting house, was, however, refused. Luke Clayton died suddenly in 1674 and was buried at Greasbrough.

Nonconformity and dissent had now become a permanent strand of the town's religious life. Despite the attempts of the established Church and government to enforce uniformity of worship with the Conventicles Act of 1664, the Five Mile Act of 1665 and the Test Act of 1673. Presbyterian ministers continued to preach and found a ready audience at meetings in private houses or hired rooms. Oliver Heywood, one of the foremost nonconformist ministers of his day, visited Rotherham on a number of occasions. Rotherham became a prominent Dissenting centre with families such as the Westbys, Staniforths, Spencers, Gills and Brights supporting Presbyterian preachers. The town's nonconformists initially met for a weekday lecture in a room on the west side of Ratten

Row (now Church Street) belonging to Mr Langley. The congregation soon outgrew this room and moved to larger premises in Millgate where, at the end of the century, the weekday 'lectures' were replaced by Sunday meetings, a direct challenge to the parish church whose congregations must have suffered. The Rev. John Mandeville (vicar 1701–4) prevailed on the owner to let the premises to someone else. The Dissenters, however, found new, larger premises with no difficulty.

Rotherham had no resident Dissenting minister after the death of Luke Clayton until John Heywood, son of Oliver. Ordained at Craven in 1681, he initially came to the Rotherham area in 1684 as tutor to the son of Thomas Westby of Ravenfield. The Westbys with their tutor were frequent visitors to the meetings in Rotherham, which, since the deaths of Shaw and Clayton, had been served by ejected ministers from Sheffield and the tutors and students from the Attercliffe Academy. On 14 March 1693 John Haywood was appointed as regular minister to the meetings, although he continued to live at Ravenfield. He remained there until 1695 when he accepted a call to serve at Pontefract (WRY). The Rev. John Rastrick, formerly vicar of Kirton, near Boston (Lin) replaced him at Rotherham.

The parish church continued to minister to the majority of the inhabitants of the parish. The church received some assistance from Parliament via the Yorkshire Committee for the Sequestration of Delinquents' Estates. In the 1640s there were approximately 3,000 communicants within the parish and the vicar's only income was his stipend of £30 13s 4d. The committee resolved in April 1646 that the sum of £46 a year was to be paid out of the tithes of the rectory of Rotherham which had belonged to Francis Stringer, gent., a delinquent, and should be used to pay an assistant minister in the parish church. They further ordered that £30 taken from the income of the prebend of Southwell's lands at Rawmarsh should be used to augment the vicar's stipend. In 1649 deans, chapters and prebends having been abolished by Parliament, the trustees for the sale of dean and chapter lands were ordered to arrange the payment of money due to the Rev. Luke Clayton or to his assistant Edward Parkes. The following year there was a complaint from the Southwell tenants in Rawmarsh that the Rotherham churchwardens had distrained them for half a year's rent and they had then had a demand for the same rent from trustees for the sale of dean and chapter lands. These two payments will have stopped on the restoration of Charles II in 1660.

The hearth tax returns of 1672 give us a picture of the town at that time. Every householder was charged at the rate of 2s per hearth unless they were exempt on the grounds of poverty. The returns for Rotherham list a total of 245 properties of which 35 are noted as 'poor' and 14 empty. Most of the properties had between one and four hearths. The largest house in the town was that inhabited by Lionel Copley with 14 hearths. There is no indication of the position of the various properties but Copley's is listed as 'per Collidge', so he may have been occupying part of the College of Jesus. The second largest house was Mr Laxton's with ten hearths, followed by Francis Mounteney's house on the High Street with nine. There are entries for the Parsonage (six hearths) and the Vicarage (five hearths). Smithies are recorded at 14 properties and the mill and common oven (one hearth each) were in the hands of Mr Mandevile. At Kimberworth there were 118 properties with 20 recorded as poor. William Hellefield or Mr Copley was occupying a 'steel Furnish' with four hearths and there were 14 smithies. The largest houses, occupied by Messrs Copley and Dawes and by Thomas Kay, had only five hearths each. Greasbrough has 87 properties recorded, 17 of them poor and two empty. The largest by far was the house of Edward Gill (Car House) with 19 hearths. There were seven smithies and a common oven in the village. Brinsworth had 21 listed properties, the largest being Mr Laughton's (Howarth Hall) with 11 hearths, followed by Valentine Hart (Ickles Hall?) with nine. The total for the whole of the ecclesiastical parish of Rotherham was 471 properties including 36 smithies. It is clear from the hearth tax that by 1672 Sheffield had outstripped Rotherham in size. In the township of Sheffield alone there were 743 properties listed, and in the whole ecclesiastical parish the total number of properties was 1,209 with 285 smithies.

The churchwardens' accounts from the late 17th century continue to be filled with items for the maintenance of the church fabric ('pointing ye battlements and collering the Leads') and for maintaining the bells. In 1675 there is an item for 'mossing the pent-house over the round Stone'. The 'round stone' was the medieval font that was placed outside the south transept during the Commonwealth. There are many entries for the purchase of food and drink for 'strange ministers' who came to preach in the parish church. There are frequent mentions of money paid to the ringers for sounding the church bells to mark important national events. The 'day of Thanksgiving for defeating the late Rebellion' (of the Duke of Monmouth) was marked in 1685. In 1688 they celebrated the news of the birth of an heir to King James II. This was James, known to history as the 'Old Pretender'. Within a year they were celebrating the news 'that the Prince of Orange wasse coming to England' and the proclamation of King William III. The bells were tolled to mark the funeral of Queen Mary in 1696, and for more joyful occasions such as the capture of Namur in 1697 and the 'tidings of peace' in 1698.

In the second half of the century the feoffees continued their task of ministering to the poor and maintaining the infrastructure of the town. The upkeep of Rotherham Bridge was a constant drain on their resources. In 1659 £23 19s 2d was spent on the repair of the bridge, 'being much decayed'. By 1681 the almshouses and the bridge were in a ruinous condition. The feoffees accepted their responsibility for the chapel but did not see why they should maintain a bridge that was used by the populace in general, not just the inhabitants of the town. In April 1681 Charles Darwent and Joseph Sorsby, on behalf of the feoffees, appeared at the Pontefract meeting of the West Riding Quarter Sessions to argue that the bridge should be the responsibility of the West Riding. The justices disputed whether the bridge was a 'riding bridge' (and therefore repairable by the county) and whether it was really necessary to maintain the roof and walls of the chapel to support the bridge. Darwent was well prepared and had been 'at great trouble and charge to search out ancient orders to show to the court'. They showed the court the feoffees' accounts to prove the sums that had been spent on the bridge over the years and were successful in their case. The justices voted the feoffees an immediate sum of £148 with grant of a further £60 and another £20 in 1682. With this money the feoffees were able to complete the necessary work on the bridge and also repair the roof and walls of the chapel. All the evidences, orders and accounts were carefully tied up by Mr Darwent and placed in the town chest 'for the better preservation thereof', but have long since disappeared.

We have a reminder of the 17th century in the town in the shape of Moorgate Hall, an early 17th-century house, remodelled by the Rotherham architect John Platt in 1768. Much of the original house survives, including the original staircase with alternate barleysugar and turned balusters. The house stood at the southern extremity of the town with the common grazing of Rotherham Moor to the south. Until the mid-18th century Moorgate

Moorgate Hall, on the southern edge of the town, was home to William West in the late 16th century and the Tooker family in the 17th century. (*Rotherham Central Library*)

Road extended only as far as the original front door of Moorgate Hall in the north front. In the late 16th century an earlier house on this site had been the home to William West, seneschal and chief steward for the Earl of Shrewsbury's south Yorkshire manors and legal adviser to the feoffees. He moved to Firbeck in 1594 and Moorgate Hall seems to have been taken over by his son Francis West. The house was bought by Charles Tooker in 1627 and remained home to the Tookers until the early 19th century. It remained a family home until 1986 and was then converted into offices.

8

Canals, Roads and Coal

The Industrial Revolution

At the opening of the 18th century Rotherham was a market town with some industry on its outskirts. By the close of the century it had become an industrial town. Before it could develop to its full industrial potential, however, it was necessary to address the drawbacks in local transport. Roads of the period, fit only for strings of packhorses or slow wagons, were thick with dust in summer and ankle deep in mud in winter. They were certainly not suited to transporting large quantities of bulky raw materials and heavy industrial products. An Act of 1555 placed the responsibility for maintenance with the civil parishes through which the roads passed. Under the system of statute labour every householder was liable to four days' labour on the roads each year. The standard of maintenance was usually poor.

The easiest, quickest means of transporting heavy, bulky material was by water. The nearest river port to Rotherham was Bawtry on the river Idle, leading into the Trent and thence to the Humber. Bawtry did a brisk trade in exporting lead and millstones from Derbyshire and cutlery and other iron goods from South Yorkshire. The Don split near Thorne, one arm leading to the Trent and the other to the Aire. In 1626 the Dutchman Cornelius Vermuyden began to drain the marshes of Hatfield Chase, diverting the Don into a single channel into the Aire. This drained the Chase but led to increased flooding in the Fishlake, Snaith and Sykehouse areas. The inhabitants forced Vermuyden to spend £20,000 cutting the Dutch river to the Ouse at Goole. After the sluice gates at Goole were carried away by floods in 1688 and not replaced, vessels up to 30 tons could reach Fishlake and small craft could reach Doncaster for three-quarters of the year. Larger craft could reach the town on flood tides. There was no navigation above Doncaster.

Various attempts between 1691 and 1704 to make the Don navigable, supported by Rotherham interests, were defeated by the vested interests of landowners, mill owners and the Trent traders. The project was not revived until the 1720s. Sheffield and the Cutlers' Company were in favour of improving navigation as a means of easing both the import of raw materials and the export of finished goods from the town. The Duke of Norfolk, however, feared damage to his water-powered industries and to his lands. In 1721 Rotherham was rumoured to be joining with Sheffield to promote a Bill. In late 1721 Doncaster, Sheffield and Rotherham were negotiating and on 1 October 1722 a meeting at Rotherham agreed to have a survey made of the river by William Palmer. His plan suggested a mixture of side cuts with improved sections of river, including a cut from Sheffield to Attercliffe Forge and another from Carbrook to Tinsley. Nearer Rotherham a cut left the river at Jordan, running to the Holmes Slitting Mill and north of the Holmes Tail Goit to Rotherham, rejoining the river at Eastwood. On 14 December 1722 the Cutlers' Company and the Corporation submitted a petition to the

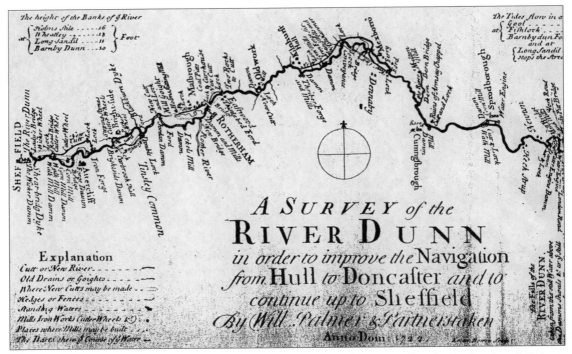

The Rotherham section of Palmer's survey of the River Don, 1722. The plan shows the site of Holmes Slitting Mill and the situation of Thistlebed Ford at Eastwood. (*Rotherham Central Library*)

Commons for leave to bring in a Bill only to see it defeated in Committee. Their opponents were sceptical of the claim that the navigation would enable pit coal to be supplied at cheaper prices than sea coal from the north-east, and claimed that Mr Gill of Car House was supporting the plan because it would raise the price of his coal by 12*d* a load.

By August 1723 Sheffield and Doncaster were negotiating to introduce another petition, abandoning any attempt to build a canal between Sheffield and Tinsley where there would be the greatest impact on existing industries. Other landowners were coming to the conclusion that the navigation was inevitable and moved from outright opposition to obtaining clauses to safeguard their interests. In March 1726 the Cutlers' Company presented their petition for a Bill to make the Don navigable from Holmstile, below Doncaster, up to Tinsley. The Bill received its third reading on 6 May. The Cutlers' Company was made responsible for making a navigation for 20-ton boats and for making and maintaining a road from Tinsley to Sheffield. The chief restrictive clause prohibited the making of new weirs and any locks would, therefore, have to be at an existing weir. They were not to make any cuts above Rotherham Bridge without giving security to Lord Frederick Howard for any damage done to his Rotherham mills and ensuring that the flow into the goit from Jordan Dam to the slitting mill at the Holmes was not diminished. In 1727 Doncaster Corporation secured an act to improve the river downstream from Holmstile to Wilsic House. The two enterprises operated separately until 1731 when they decided to amalgamate. This required another Act, passed in 1733, to establish the Company of Proprietors of the Navigation of the river Don. They were empowered to make a new cut from Bromley Sands, above Rotherham High Dam, to Ickles Dam.

In March 1731 stone and timber had been ordered at Hooton Roberts and Dalton to construct the lock and bridge at Aldwarke that was to remain the head of navigation for some years. Warehouses were constructed at Swinton and Aldwarke in 1733. In August 1738 preparations were being made to complete the cut to Rotherham High Dam, and in 1740 the navigation reached Rotherham through a cut that left the river at Eastwood and ran parallel with the north bank, returning to the river above Rotherham weir. The navigation then followed the river, past the confluence with the Rother, to Bromley Sands where it entered Bromley Sands Lock, constructed in 1742. A short cut took it above Ickles Weir. After a short stretch of river, Deadman's Hole Lock and cut bypassed the loop of the Don past Jordan Weir. In 1751 the navigation reached Tinsley where warehouses and wharves were constructed. In 1765 new warehouses were built at Rotherham and Swinton and the company embarked on a policy of controlling the mills along the river, beginning by leasing the mills at Doncaster and Aldwarke. This was to allow them to control the amount of water abstracted by the mills and so ensure that sufficient remained to keep the navigation at a usable level. By 1769 30,000 tons of coal annually was being transported along the navigation from the collieries around Rotherham for sale in Gainsborough, Lincoln and Newark. In that year an abortive scheme was proposed to make the Rother navigable from Chesterfield (Dby) to Rotherham as a rival to the proposed Chesterfield Canal from Chesterfield to the Trent at Stockwith (Ntt). This canal opened in 1777 and took some trade from the Don. It also spelled the end of Bawtry as a port. In 1779–80 the Marquess of Rockingham employed William Jessop to construct a private branch canal from the Don Navigation at Parkgate to Cinder Bridge to serve the collieries on his estate around Greasbrough. This had four locks in its length of 1½ miles.

Although the Don Navigation greatly assisted the transport of raw materials and finished goods, it was still necessary to take the goods to and from the canal by road. In the early 18th century English roads were reputed to be the worst in Europe. When the Earl of Oxford passed through Rotherham in 1725, his coach was able to average only 2 mph. At the same period it could take eight days to travel 209 miles from York to London. It was finally accepted that charging tolls was the only way to provide the funds to keep main roads in

The Don Navigation downstream of Rotherham Lock. The original cut turned right here into the Don. Between 1835 and 1865 the navigation ran straight on beneath the photographer. The present Central station, on the line of the Great Central line opened in 1868, can be seen at the left. (*Author*)

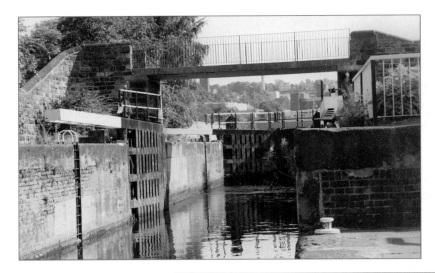

The present Rotherham Lock. (*Author*)

A lightly loaded barge being hauled along the Rotherham Cut in the 1930s. The smoking chimneys at the left mark the power station on Rawmarsh Road. The tall chimney belongs to the Refuse Destructor. (*Rotherham Central Library*)

repair, and the turnpike trusts came into operation. The first trust proper was set up in 1706 to improve Watling Street (now the A5) between Fornhill (Bdf) and Stony Stratford (Bkm). By 1770 over 500 trusts had been created, covering 15,000 miles of road. Between 1754 and 1770 the journey time between London and Edinburgh fell from 10 days to 4 days.

The first road in south Yorkshire to be turnpiked was the ancient salt route from Cheshire. The Act for the road from Stockport to Woodhead was passed in 1732. In 1740 an Act was passed to deal with the road from the county boundary at Saltersbrook to Barnsley and Doncaster with a branch from Hartcliffe Hill, south-west of Penistone, to Rotherham, included at the instigation of the Cutlers' Company. In the words of the Act, 'the Roads leading from Doncaster and Rotherham . . . to Manchester . . . are publick Highways and very convenient for conveying goods from the Eastern to the Western Seas' but sections of the roads from 'Rotherham to Hartcliffe Hill . . . have for several Years past been very bad and are now dangerous'. From Hartcliffe Hill the road ran to Chapeltown, across Thorpe Common (on the line of the present A629), and down Old Wortley Road

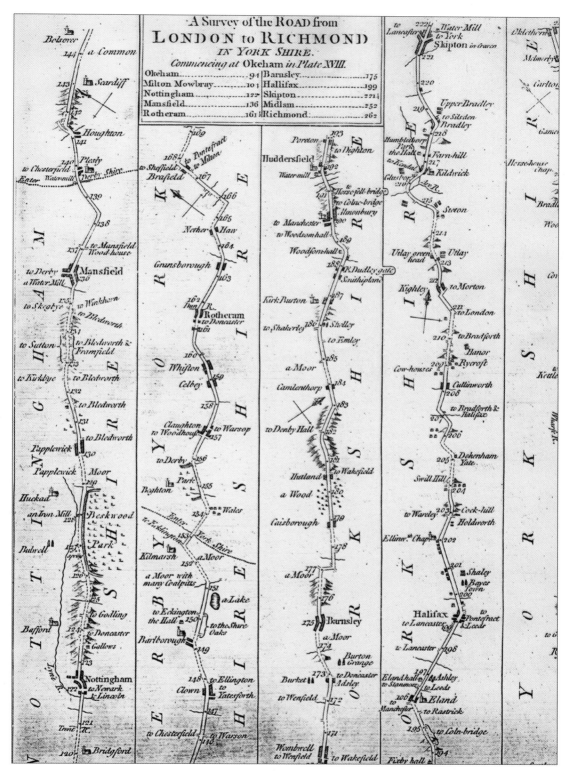

John Ogilby's map of the road from London to Richmond (1675) showing the road passing into Yorkshire between Killamarsh and Wales and running via Rotherham Bridge and Greasbrough towards Barnsley. (*Rotherham Central Library*)

The Rotherham area from Jeffrey's Map of Yorkshire (1771) showing the turnpike roads radiating from the town. The figures alongside the roads (e.g. 1/21) mark the position of milestones.

through Kimberworth village. At Rotherham the road connected with the newly completed Don Navigation where salt from Cheshire, textiles from Lancashire and iron goods from Wortley Forge could be transferred to barges. The tolls paid by travellers varied according to the type of wagon or carriage and were graded to take account of the wear on the road caused by various types of conveyance. On the Rotherham to Hartcliffe Hill road coaches pulled by four horses paid 1s, by two horses 6d and by one horse 4d. Wagons, except those carrying corn, wood, timber, bark or coal, paid 1s if pulled by six horses and 3d if pulled by one or two. If they were carrying corn, wood etc. they paid only 6d for six horses and 3d if drawn by four or fewer. Droves of cattle paid 10d per score (20) and droves of calves or sheep paid 5d per score. There was a tollhouse at the bottom of Bradgate Lane.

The Rotherham and Pleasley Road received its Act in 1764. The feoffees contributed £100 towards the expenses of the Act, for a new turnpike would free them from paying the annual chiminage money to the Duke of Norfolk. The duke, however, still demanded his annual payment and the feoffees finally bought out the rent in 1788 for a lump sum payment of £25. The road did not follow the traditional route from the town centre towards Whiston but travelled up Mansfield Road into Moorgate Road and cut a new route across Rotherham Moor, bypassing Moorgate Hall, to meet up with the old road near the Mile Oak. At Whiston crossroads it crossed the Tinsley and Bawtry turnpike of 1760, continuing south through Swallownest to Clowne (Dby), now the A618, to meet the Chesterfield and Mansfield turnpike at Pleasley (Dby). At Swallownest the road crossed the Attercliffe and Worksop turnpike (1764) giving access to Lincoln and Newark (Ntt). The first tollhouse out of Rotherham stood near the Mile Oak and there was another controlling Whiston crossroads. North of Rotherham the obvious route would have been to follow the old road to Barnsley via Greasbrough and Wombwell, which was in poor condition. However, the Marquess of Rockingham used his influence to divert the route through his own estate to meet the Sheffield, Barnsley and Wakefield Turnpike (1758) at Hood Hill. There were toll gates at Rotherham, Cinder Bridge (north of Greasbrough), Nether Haugh and Wentworth, where the toll house still exists at the west end of the village.

The other main route, from Tinsley through Rotherham to Doncaster, also gained its Act in 1764. The advantages of adequate roads were not lost on local industrialists and Rotherham ironmaster Samuel Walker thought it worth investing £10 towards the costs of the Bill. He was one of the trustees of the road and the Act contained a clause exempting any horse or carriage coming on to the road from the Walkers' works at Masbrough via the ford at Deadman's Hole from paying tolls at any gate between Tinsley and Rotherham. The Tinsley and Doncaster Trust was a continuation of the Sheffield to Tinsley road, turnpiked in 1759. The road as originally proposed would have bypassed Thrybergh and Hooton Roberts had not the inhabitants petitioned the Marquess of Rockingham. As Hooton Roberts was part of the Marquess' estates and the road from Wentworth joined the Doncaster Road there, he was able to use his influence to have the original line restored. There was a tollgate at the eastern end of Doncaster Road where the tollhouse, with its typical bow window to allow the collector to see in both directions, survived as a dwelling until 1958.

A number of milestones remain in the Rotherham area. Early milestones were in stone with incised inscriptions. Later stones bore cast-iron plates. One can be seen on Moorgate Road against the wall in front of Thomas Rotherham College, informing the traveller that it is 1 mile to College Square, Rotherham, 19½ miles to Pleasley and 22¼ miles to Mansfield. There is another stone a mile further down the road. On the Tinsley to Doncaster road, at the end of Deadman's Hole Lane, Templeborough, the original incised stone has been turned round and a new cast-iron inscription fixed to what had been the back.

Changes in trade patterns could have a devastating effect on the fortunes of individual roads and the road from Hartcliffe Hill was an early victim. The move of the head of navigation from Aldwarke and Rotherham to Tinsley in 1751 and the turnpiking of the road from Sheffield to Sparrow Pit (Dby) to join the main London to Manchester road diverted much of its trade and the trust became insolvent in 1762. A new trust was sanctioned in

The toll house, Broom Road, on the Barnby Moor Turnpike, just before it was demolished in 1908. (*Rotherham Central Library*)

1788 to deal with the road from Rotherham as far as Four Lane Ends, south of Wortley. The impetus for creating turnpikes continued into the early years of the 19th century. Thomas Jeffrey's Map of Yorkshire (1772) shows no direct road between Rotherham and Rawmarsh, travellers having to make their way via Greasbrough and Scrooby Lane or via the Doncaster road and Aldwarke to Parkgate. It was not until 1808 that the direct road via Parkgate and Rawmarsh to Swinton was turnpiked, straightening the original winding lanes connecting the villages. The road from Wentworth to Hooton Roberts was turnpiked in 1818, largely at the expense of Earl Fitzwilliam. Finally, in 1826, the road from Wellgate via Broom Road and Wickersley Road to the Brecks was turnpiked as part of the Rotherham and Barnby Moor Trust, to give a more direct route from Rotherham to Maltby, Bawtry and the Great North Road. The tollhouse on Broom Road survived as a dwelling until 1908.

The network of improved turnpike roads led to a great increase in public transport in the shape of long-distance coaches, while coaching inns sprang up to serve the needs of the coaches and the passengers they carried. Carriers, who established regular services between the towns and the surrounding villages, met more local transport needs. In Rotherham the main coaching inn was the Crown on the High Street. A service from London to Sheffield was begun in April 1760 and extended to Leeds in May. Other services ran along the Great North Road via Doncaster. Rotherham initially had no direct services but in 1787 a light coach was being advertised between Sheffield and Doncaster four days a week, calling at the Crown, connecting at Doncaster with coaches to London, York and Hull. The fare from Rotherham to Doncaster was 4s 0d. In the early 19th century the mail coach from Sheffield to Doncaster, via Rotherham, was taking 1½ hours on its journey and the Sheffield to Scarborough coach, run during the bathing season, took 15 hours. In 1829 coaches ran from the Crown to Doncaster, Lincoln, Louth (Lin), Sheffield, Manchester and Thorne and a carrier's cart, with passenger accommodation, ran weekly from Sheffield to Swinton and Wath.

The arrival of the Don Navigation enabled coal to be transported in bulk outside the local market. By the early 1750s south Yorkshire coal was finding a market in the Humber estuary and in the Trent valley, competing with coal brought by sea from Durham. In the 1760s coal from the pits around Rotherham found a ready sale as far south as Newark (Ntt) and in the Lincoln area. Coal from the mines on the Wentworth Estate was marketed in the Malton area of the East Riding via the Ouse and the Derwent Navigation, controlled by the Marquess of Rockingham. The coal traffic on the Don in 1772 was estimated at 40,000 wagon loads (c. 80,000 tons). The canals also encouraged other industries, particularly iron and steelworking and brickmaking, all of which used coal as a fuel. The growth in the industry in the 18th century is shown by the increased rental that coal owners were able to demand from the entrepreneurs who worked the seams. When John Hirst leased collieries at Swinton and Greasbrough from the Wentworth estate in 1723, he paid a combined rent of £200 a year. In 1736 William Spencer of Bramley Grange agreed to get the coal at Barbot Hall, Greasbrough Fields, Kimberworth and Ginhouse Farm, employing 12 'getters' at Kimberworth and Ginhouse and no more than 6 men at Barbot Hall and Greasbrough Fields at rents of £252 and £126 a year respectively. John Bowdon of Beightonfields (Dby) took over both collieries at the same rent in 1742, just as the navigation reached Rotherham. Production at the Greasbrough Colliery rose so rapidly that the rent was raised to £240. The Parkgate seam at Bassingthorpe, Kimberworth, owned by the Wentworth Estate, was leased to Thomas and William Fenton in 1757 on a 21-year lease, paying £324 for the first two years and £648 for the remainder of the term. The Fentons were the largest coal masters in

Two small collieries at Car House, shown on T. Harris's engraved view of Rotherham, *c.* 1740. (*Rotherham Central Library*)

the 18th-century West Riding, with extensive interests further north in addition to Greasbrough. In the 1770s a total of some 166,393 wagon loads of coal (*c.* 366,000 tons) were sent down the Don from the Fenton pits at Greasbrough.

Mining has always been a dangerous occupation and the 18th century, with its primitive safety precautions, was no exception. We have a record of the dangers in a pamphlet entitled *Dispensations of divine providence illustrated in brief narratives of the many distressing deaths which have occurred at the Greasbrough Colliery 1762–1823* by Paul Rodgers. The first death at the colliery was David Pattrick, killed in a pit on the east side of Bassingthorpe Spring in 1762 'by a large piece of clod falling upon him from the roof'. Elias Broadhead, a boy of 10 or 12, fell down a shaft in a close called Cliff Riddings and George Stringer was 11 years old when he was putting a corf (tub) on the rope at a pit above Wingfield and a gust of wind blew him down the 100 yd shaft. Abraham Mellors was only 10 when he fell down a shaft while attempting to attach a rope. Some accidents were caused by sheer stupidity. William Knapten had a day off in 1772 when his pit was 'at play' but chose, with a companion, Joseph Thompson, to enter a working pit by sliding down the rope. Both boys fell, Knapten being killed and Thompson breaking both legs. Two 13-year-olds, Joseph Mercer and Jeremiah Pollard, eager to get to the surface at the end of their shift in Quarry Close Pit, above Lapwater, hitched a lift on a loaded corf. The rope broke, precipitating corf and boys to the shaft bottom. Firedamp was a constant hazard, through explosion or suffocation. Joseph Hobson, aged 16 or 17, ventured with a lighted candle into a dangerous part of the pit in pursuit of a rat and set off the gas with fatal results. Underground fires were frequent. In 1779 William Craven, underground steward at the colliery, entered a pit near Wingfield to inspect a fire that had been burning for some time.

On reaching the surface again 'the effect of being so long in the damp seized him', and he fell back down the shaft. It was with great difficulty that two men were persuaded to descend the shaft to retrieve the body. They had barely returned to the surface when the damp ignited.

The technology of mining had progressed from the medieval bell pit, but the seams worked were still shallow and it took little capital to set up as a miner. Even in the third quarter of the century the Fenton's pits at Bassingthorpe were mostly only 25 yd deep. Although the Fenton workings were generally known as Greasbrough Colliery they consisted of a large number of short-lived pits sunk close together. It was cheaper to win the coal by sinking numerous shafts from the surface, rather than driving long headings underground. The coal was wound out of the pits by horse-powered gins – a horizontal wooden drum supported over the shaft driven by a horse walking round in circles. Two such gins are shown in the foreground of an engraved view of Rotherham from Car House, published c. 1740. The Fentons had four shafts at work at Bassingthorpe in 1765, rising to ten in 1776 when the whole area was covered by filled in shafts. Problems with water could be solved by the use of a 'fire engine' or steam engine of the Newcomen type to drive pumps. The earliest in South Yorkshire seems to be that installed at Car House, Greasbrough, by William Spencer under the terms of his 1735 lease, to drain the seams at Car House 'as well as those lying within the Precincts of Kimberworth as those coals also which lye within Greasborough Bierley'. The engine was intended to raise water from the Thick Coal 70 yards to a sough driven to the Don. Three fire engine owners are listed at Greasbrough in 1763. The Fentons installed a Newcomen engine at Bassingthorpe to drain the mine to a depth of 80 yd.

The Hirst family of Clough had worked pits at Meadowbank in the middle of the century and acquired a steam engine to drain their workings near Darley Common. The Walkers sank pits to supply coal to their ironworks at the Holmes. The hillside above the Holmes was not a geologically fortunate area for coal workings as it lay between two faults and the coal seams dipped steeply to the east. Pits were sunk to three seams and a sough was driven to carry off water to the Don. A Newcomen engine was installed to drain the pits in 1777. Mining was also carried out in the Herringthorpe area to the south-east of Rotherham. As early as 1702 Edward Fretwell of Wickersley entered into a seven-year agreement with the Earl of Arundel to extract coal on wasteland at Herringthorpe, then in the manor of Whiston.

Although the Don Navigation allowed coal to be carried in bulk, the coal still had to be moved from the pithead to the canal wharf. It became common to link colliery and canal with a wooden railway or tramway on which coal wagons could be pulled by horses or oxen. First developed in the Tyne Valley, they were frequently referred to as 'Newcastle Roads'. By 1763 the Fentons had a 3-mile wooden tramway linking their pits at Bassingthorpe with a canal wharf near the site of the present Beatson Clark works. By 1766 the wooden rails were strengthened with iron plates. In Bassingthorpe Spring several branches of the tramway served the various pits within the wood – Webster Pit (or Fourth Hill Pit), Fourth Wood Pit, Wards Pit, Steel Pit, Second Hill Pit, Third Wood Pit, Water Pit, Long Ridge Pit, and First Wood Pit. The Bassingthorpe tramway became increasingly crowded when mining extended north to the Whitegate area of Greasbrough. It was largely to ease this congestion that the Marquess of Rockingham had the Greasbrough Canal built. A tramroad connected the canal with the engine house at Squirrel Castle and the Whitegate Colliery. Traces of these tramroads can still be seen in Bassingthorpe Spring. The tramroads continued in use until the 1830s when the Fenton collieries closed. To the west of Rotherham a short tramroad connected the Walkers' pits at Garrowtree with the canal to the west of the Holmes.

9

Sad Irons and Cannon

The Walker Ironworks

Jonathan (1711–78), Samuel (1715–82) and Aaron Walker (1718–77) were the sons by his second wife of Joseph Walker (1678–1729), farmer and nailer of Stubbin House, Grenoside. Samuel became master of Grenoside Endowed School, supplementing his income by undertaking surveying and making sundials. Jonathan took over the family farm while Aaron took over the nailing business and undertook agricultural work when trade was slack. One of the few records left by the Walkers is a manuscript diary or journal started by Samuel Walker and continued by other hands after his death. The original of a short version of the journal, covering the years up to 1760, a facsimile of which was published by John Guest in his *Historic notices of Rotherham* (1879), is held in the Archives & Local Studies Section of Rotherham Central Library, inserted into Guest's own, extra-illustrated copy of his *Historic notices of men and manufactures . . .* (1865). Alfred O. Walker published a longer version of the journal in 1879, detailing the history of the enterprises year by year. The original of this journal is

A portrait of Samuel Walker I (1715–82). (*Rotherham Central Library*)

lost but Walker's account was the basis of A.H. John's 1951 book *Minutes relating to Messrs Samuel Walker and Co., Rotherham. . . .* A second, original copy of the journal is among the archives of the Institute of Mechanical Engineers.

In 1741, with the nail trade in decline, Aaron began to look for a more stable occupation. Together with John Crawshaw he began experimenting with 'a tryal of foundering', melting iron in crucible pots using Abraham Booth's smithy in Oughtibridge Lane. The experiments were unsuccessful until a reverberatory or 'air' furnace was erected in the smithy behind Samuel's cottage. They were able to produce small iron objects, mostly smoothing irons and bushes for cartwheels. The following year they produced 5 tons of goods, rising to 10 tons in 1743. Although still the schoolmaster, Samuel was spending as much time as possible on the business and John Crawshaw was employed as needed at 12*d* a day. A new foundry, with two air furnaces and a smithy, was erected in 1744. In 1745, when production rose to 39 tons, Samuel gave up the school and built himself a house. The following year saw the capital of the business valued at £600. The stock was valued at £400 while Jonathan provided £100 and Samuel Walker and John Crawshaw invested £50 each.

The opportunities for expansion at Grenoside were limited and Samuel must have foreseen a day when far larger castings would need to be moved. The new navigation at Rotherham offered easier and cheaper transport. With the increase in production Samuel 'began to see ye disadvantage of being so far from ye navigable river' and decided to move the business to Masbrough. The works at Grenoside were not abandoned but continued in use and were even expanded. The Walkers leased a site off Masbrough Street, Masbrough, in 1746, erecting two reverberatory furnaces, a casting house and a smithy. Aaron moved to Masbrough to supervise the operations and a new house was built for him adjoining the foundry in 1747. The business expanded in 1748 when Samuel Walker entered into a partnership with John Booth, a prosperous yeoman nailer and leading nail chapman, to erect a steel furnace. This would have been a reverberatory furnace, producing blister steel. Although the Walker enterprise is often thought of as a single enterprise, the steel business was always a separate partnership. Samuel Walker built himself a house 'above the steel furnace', moving in November 1749.

One of the early lines of the company was cooking pots requiring a special grade of iron, much harder and more brittle. By 1751 they were making over 200 tons of castings a year and the value of stock was assessed at £3,000. The years 1753 and 1754 saw the company build two keels, called *Providence* and *Industry*, to carry their goods on the navigation. In 1754 they leased a plot of land on the riverbank at Masbrough between the Don and the

An extract from the original, short version, of the Walker Journal, referred to in the text. (*Rotherham Central Library*)

Some fragments still remain on the site, off Chapel Walk at Masbrough, where the Walkers established their first works in 1746. (*Author*)

canal from the Earl of Effingham, as the site for a new water-powered forge. Samuel Walker and John Crawshaw each put £400 into the company in 1754, increasing the capital to £5,600. The partnership was divided into 14 shares, of which Samuel held six, Aaron four and Jonathan and John Crawshaw two each.

In 1758 they expanded on to the site of the Holmes Slitting Mill, a mile from the Masbrough works. Here there was also a blast furnace and rolling mill, all driven by waterpower from the Holmes Goit, leased from the Earl of Effingham. There was a flurry of activity adapting the buildings and machinery and preparing the new site for business. Another lease in 1760 covered the site of grinding and boring mills, built in 1759–60. The slitting and rolling mills were rebuilt and the blast furnace and associated works refurbished. Coal and ironstone mines were opened to feed the works. A navigable cut was made from the Holmes to the Don above Ickles Mill to give access to the Navigation. The collieries opened at this time were at Garrowtree, on the valley side above the Holmes. The charcoal

The former Ebenezer Chapel on Chapel Walk (now a mosque) was erected on the site of Samuel Walker's Masbrough Hall, his second house at Masbrough. It stood only a few yards from the Walkers' Masbrough works. (*Author*)

Samuel Walker's house, Masbrough Hall, erected in 1768–9, painted by Christopher Thomson in 1867, shortly before it was demolished. (*Rotherham Central Library*)

blast furnace was returned to blast. The stack of the furnace was raised in 1766 to enable output to be increased. It was joined by a second blast furnace in 1767 and a third in 1770. In 1771 the second furnace had its stack heightened to enable it to use coke as a fuel. In 1782 the Holmes estate was purchased outright. The purchase, for £14,500, was negotiated by Samuel Walker but was not completed until August 1782, after his death.

In the 1760s the Walkers fought a prolonged legal battle with the Don Navigation over the abstraction of water in excess of their rights. The Walkers wished to obtain preferential tolls in return for keeping sufficient water in the navigation. The partners offered to pass sufficient water though a new cut from the works to keep Ickles Dam full, in return for preferential tolls on the whole navigation, complete exemption between Rotherham and the Holmes and £60 annually. In 1763 the Walkers leased the water rights at Thrybergh, enabling them to paralyse the navigation below Rotherham. They offered to stop the works when water was low in return for reduced tolls between Rotherham and Thrybergh and a payment of £25 p.a. towards the maintenance of the river. Both proposals were rejected and in 1770 the Walkers completely stopped navigation in the Long Cut at Thrybergh. When another 30 boats were stranded in October 1770, the Navigation had to admit defeat and pay the Walkers £90 a year plus exemption from tolls between Rotherham and the Holmes.

At Thrybergh in 1763 they took a lease for 42 years, from the Hon. Mrs Elizabeth Finch of Thrybergh Hall, of the existing iron forge and fulling mill on the Don, with authority to build other forges, tilt hammers and grinding wheels. According to the Journal they rebuilt the forge and added four dwellings, carpenters' and smiths' shops and a charcoal yard. The Thrybergh site was remote from the village and much of the workforce seems to have lived on the site. In 1770 the partners took a lease from the Duke of Leeds of a site at Burcroft, Conisbrough, where they erected a grinding wheel and boring mill, used for boring cannon. In the same year there is reference to a new tilt, built at the 'Sand Bed', the bed of gravel in the Don adjoining the Town Mill in Rotherham.

A proper valuation of the partnership's value taken in 1765 put it at £28,000. In the 1760s dividends of between £210 and £350 were being divided between the partners each year, but there was usually a proviso that it be paid 'as soon as there is cash to spare'. A new steel furnace was erected at the Yellands in 1766. Morley suggests that this was probably the first crucible steel furnace erected by the Walkers. This is confirmed by the 1773 entry in the journal referring to the Yellands furnace as a 'casting steel furnace'. Only the crucible process could produce molten steel for casting. Four extra crucible furnaces and a coking oven were added in that year. The company acquired its first 'fire engine' or steam engine in 1777. This was an atmospheric engine of the Newcomen type, with a cylinder of 72 in diameter and a 6-ft stroke, installed to pump water out of the colliery at Garrow Tree, near the top of Rutland Street. The engine house was later converted into a dwelling and survived until at

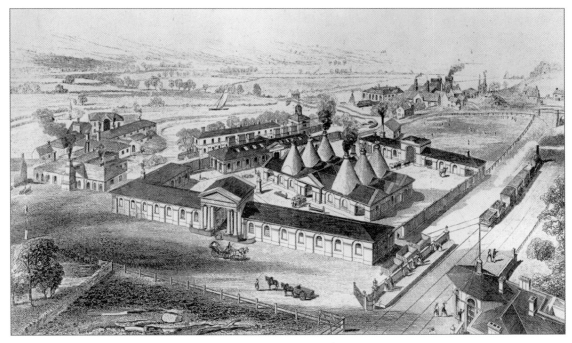

Peter Stubs Warrington Works was erected on the site of Holmes Hall. The Walkers' Holmes Works (later Habershons) can be seen at the left (with the stepped chimney). The Walkers' blast furnace site lies in the background with Holmes station in the foreground. (*Rotherham Central Library*)

The engine house at Garrowtree, Masbrough, which housed the Walkers' first 'fire engine', purchased in 1777. The building was later converted into a cottage and survived until the 1940s. (*Rotherham Central Library*)

least 1945. A second steam engine was installed at the Holmes Furnaces in 1781–2 to provide blast for between three and six months a year when the river was too low to use waterpower. This was a more modern design than Boulton and Watts' patent, many of the castings being produced at Masbrough.

As the business grew the Walkers' works became something of a visitor attraction and a number of visitors recorded their impressions. When Arthur Young visited Rotherham as part of his *Six months tour through the North of England* in the late 1760s, he wrote:

Rotherham is famous for its ironworks, of which it contains one very large one, belonging to Mr Walker, and one or two smaller. Near the town are two collieries, out of which iron ore is dug, as well as the coals to work it with; these collieries and works employ near 500 hands. The ore is here worked into metal and then into bar iron, and the bars sent to Sheffield to be worked, and to all parts of the country; this is one branch of their business. Another is the foundry, to which they run the ore into metal pigs, and then cast it into all sorts of boilers, pans, plough-shares etc. etc. etc. . . . .

Besides the iron manufactory, they have a pottery in which is made the white cream-coloured [Staffordshire] and tortoise-shell earthen-ware: It employs about two or three and twenty men and 40 boys. . . .

The pottery referred to was on the banks of the Don, at the bottom of Domine Lane, and was run in conjunction with the Rotherham architect John Platt who entered into a partnership with Samuel Walker II in December 1766. The partnership advertised 'white stoneware, black tortoise shell, agate, cream Colour, also gilt enamel ware for tea and table services at reasonable rates'. Samuel Walker bought out his son and John Platt in 1772, paying them £316 10s each. The property was described as 'a messuage, barns, ovens, furnaces, warehouses etc., near Domine Well', with the stock of finished and unfinished earthenware, clay, coals, engines, debts due, the flint mill in Don Close and the unexpired terms of 13 apprentices. The 1774 plan of Rotherham shows two furnaces on the site. In 1794 the pottery was sold to Richard and William Stanley, partners with the Walkers in the bank, Walkers, Eyre and Stanley. The works may have been out of production by this date as it is described as being divided into several dwellings. By 1825 the site was described as 'commonly called the pottery' but part of the site had been converted into an iron foundry.

General iron goods such as sad irons (smoothing irons), frying pans and cooking pots made up the bulk of the company's production. In 1772, out of a total production of

The cannon of the Walkers and the sheaves of Sheffield above the door to the Royal Bank of Scotland at the bottom of the High Street, erected in 1892 on the site of the Walkers' private bank. (*Author*)

682 tons, 101 tons were sad irons. Of 91 tons of sad irons produced in 1775, 58 tons were sent to London and 33 tons sold elsewhere. The year 1774 sees the first mention of the production of cannon at Masbrough. The casting of cannon was a very exacting and precise science and in 1775 the Board of Ordnance ordered that in future all cannon were to be cast solid and bored out after casting. Once out of the mould the barrels would be taken to the water-powered boring mill where the bore would be bored while the outside was turned. This had to be done with the utmost accuracy. The barrel then had to be proofed. This involved accurate gauging of the bore and the external measurements followed by trial firings with pre-measured charges and shot and a thorough inspection for any flaws or cracks. A German visitor, Johanna Schopenhauer, visited the works in the early years of the 19th century and watched the casting and turning of cannon at the Holmes:

We had the good fortune to see a 24-pound cannon being cast. The liquid metal flowed from two furnaces into two channels, banked up with earth and sand. They soon joined into a single channel from which a steady flow of molten metal filled a deep-set mould. . . . We were also permitted to watch a cannon being bored, for they are, of course, cast solid. This used to be a secret operation but it was showed to us when we expressed a desire to see it. The machinery used for this purpose is driven by water. A long iron rod, the thickness of the required muzzle of the cannon, is placed in a horizontal position. On the end of the rod is a flat, thin piece of steel with sharp ends, shaped like tongues. The cannon, driven by water with incredible power, is forced to rotate, winding itself round the rod, allowing the rod to polish the inside of the bore smoothly and evenly.

In preparation for the manufacture of cannon, a new casting house, two boring houses, with pit, cranes, stove room and three furnaces were constructed at the Holmes in 1774. The first year of production saw 40 tons of cannon produced, rising to 405 tons in 1776. Annual production climbed steadily, reaching 872 tons in 1780 and 1,220 tons in 1781 before falling to 1,039 tons in 1782. Demand obviously fell sharply with the end of the American War of Independence in 1783 when only 214 tons of cannon were recorded.

The Walker Cannon which now stands outside the Town Hall in the Crofts. (*Author*)

Over the same period production of general castings was steady at *c.* 800 tons a year. By May 1777 they were calculating the value of the company at £102,500 'tho' this may be thot too high; but when we consider the quantity of Guns made this year, and the good success therein, and the interest for money lent, etc., there seems good reason for the above supposition'. Another £24,500 was divided between the partners in 1778.

Sadly the journal stops recording annual tonnages after 1783, possibly because Samuel Walker died on 12 May 1782 and the journal was taken over by another hand. He was the last of the three brothers to die, Aaron having died in January 1777 and Jonathan the following year. In recording the 'irreparable loss in the death of the first partner in the Firm Samuel Walker', the Journal refers to 'that integrity, industry, foresight and perseverance that appeared in all his actions'. The title of the company was changed to Samuel Walker and Co., the partners being Samuel Walker II (1742–92), Joshua Walker (1750–1815), Joseph Walker (1752–1801), Thomas Walker (1756–1828) (the sons of Samuel Walker), Jonathan Walker II (1757–87) (son of Jonathan Walker), John Walker (1760–1804) (son of Aaron Walker) and John Crawshaw. Joshua was the driving force of the new partnership. John Walker did not remain a partner for long. In 1783 his 'imprudent course of life' caused him to sell his shares to Samuel Walker II, who generously divided them with his three brothers.

An interesting insight into the partnership arrangements of the second generation and their view of business ethics is given in a small notebook, part of which was reprinted inaccurately by John Guest in 1879. The Archives & Local Studies Section of Rotherham Central Library now holds the original. The author (possibly Joshua) promotes the philosophy that every partner should be given some discrete area of responsibility so that the foremen would not become complacent and take advantage of their positions of trust. The partners had been apt to dip into the different aspects of the business as their fancy took them. The author clearly believes that profit is not the sole purpose of the business – 'surely none of my partners think the principal object in this world is money'. The 18th-century equivalent of the company car can be found in the recommendation that each partner be allowed to keep a horse at the company's expense but not to be extravagant in their buying of horseflesh. The list of partners would indicate that the notebook dates from after the retirement of John Walker in 1783. The appearance of John Rhodes, manager of the Holmes Mills, dates it to before his death in March 1784.

The Crawshaws left the business in April 1789 but the partnership was not formally dissolved until 1791, when John Crawshaw received £19,005 for his two fourteenth shares. Samuel Walker II died in 1792 and the company was reconstituted as Joshua Walker and Co. In 1801 the partners took over the running of the Milton Ironworks at Elsecar. Although cannon making features little in the journal after 1782, it remained a major part of the business. It has been estimated that the Walkers produced around 13,000 cannon between 1773 and 1815. From 1786 the company was co-operating with Capt. Thomas Blomefield, Inspector of Artillery, to improve the design of cannons. In February 1786 the company received a contract from the Officers of Ordnance to supply 1,000 tons of guns to the ordnance stores at Woolwich before 31 December 1787, to be manufactured from the best and finest iron of a close and dense texture. An account of the ordnance on board HMS *Victory* in March 1808 shows that the Walkers had provided all 28 of the 32-pounder guns, 28 out of 30 18-pounders and 23 of the 36 12-pounders. Walker cannon can still be seen on board the *Victory* at Portsmouth and others are on display at the Tower of London, Edinburgh Castle, Southsea Castle (Ham) and at numerous other sites in the British Isles and abroad. There is one on public display in Rotherham. Many muzzle-loading cannon ended up sunk into quays as mooring posts. Rotherham Metropolitan Borough Council purchased one such barrel, a 9-pounder, from a scrapyard in Kent in 1996. This now sits on a replica naval carriage outside the town hall in the Crofts.

The other business for which the Walker Works became internationally famous was the casting of iron bridges. This market opened up as a result of their association with the radical politician Thomas Paine (1732–1809), who first began to work on his design for an iron bridge while in America. In search of a wider market Paine moved to France in 1787 and, finding no interest there, returned to England. In 1788 he obtained a patent for his design (no. 1667). Searching for a foundry that could turn his design into metal, Paine approached the Walkers, writing in September 1788 to Thomas Jefferson in the USA that 'the Iron Works in Yorkshire belonging to the Walkers near to Sheffield are the most eminent in England in point of establishment and property'. Paine came up to Masbrough in October to arrange the casting, returning for a successful trial erection of the arch in April 1789. It was not, however, until the summer of 1790 that he was able to start erecting the arch on a site at Paddington, charging the public 1s each to view it. The bridge remained on view for a year and the castings were then removed to Rotherham. Paine was now distracted from his bridge designs by the outbreak of the French Revolution and the publication of his *Rights of Man* (1791), which led to his exile in France.

Their involvement with Paine was to prove invaluable for the Walkers. The company was chosen to cast the second iron bridge to be erected in England, across the River Wear at Sunderland (Dur), designed and constructed by local engineer Thomas Wilson. There were six ribs, each constructed from 105 open-frame voussoirs connected with wrought-iron bands. The completed bridge was opened on 9 August 1796. At the same period the Walkers also constructed an iron footbridge over the Don at Bridgehouses, Sheffield. This lasted until 1864 when it was swept away by the Sheffield Flood.

The Walkers went on to cast several more bridges to designs by Thomas Wilson. Their second Wilson bridge still exists and was probably the first iron bridge in the western hemisphere. It has an 83 ft span and crosses the Rio Cobre at Spanish Town, Jamaica, and was erected in 1801. The Walkers contracted, at the price of £5,560, to cast the new bridge at Yarm (Dur), erected in 1805–6. The ironwork was 'justly admired for its excellent workmanship, beautiful and improved construction and an appearance of durability'.

Unfortunately it collapsed into the river on 13 January 1806, because of failure of the abutments. No blame was attached to the Walkers. The ironwork was removed and the existing stone bridge, which is still in service today, was widened.

Wilson's next bridge, a collaboration with the engineer John Rennie, across the Whitham at Boston (Lin), was also cast at Masbrough. The span was 85 ft and the width 39 ft. The Walkers reported that the ironwork was all cast in January 1806 and the structure was virtually complete by October with the roadway finished in January 1807. A number of faults were then found in the ironwork and the opening was delayed while liability was disputed, with Rennie advising that the cracks were unimportant. The bridge accordingly opened on 2 May 1807. Despite its flaws Boston Bridge lasted until 1913, when a steel arch on Rennie's abutments replaced it. The final Wilson bridge with which the Walkers were involved, Tickford Bridge over the Ouzel at Newport Pagnell (Bkm), still carries traffic today. Opened in 1810, this has a span of 60 ft with 6 ribs of 11 segments each. The cost of the ironwork was £1,640 with an extra £103 for the carriage.

John Rennie's problems with the bridge at Boston did not prevent him from using the Walkers to cast his bridge over the Thames at Southwark, a far greater undertaking than any of the earlier bridges cast at Masbrough. A gap of 708 ft was spanned with three arches, the side arches being 210 ft each and the centre arch 240 ft, then the longest iron span in the world. The total weight of iron used was 5,308 tons with some single castings reaching 10 tons. One single piece, the pier plate at the Southwark end, weighed 19 tons and was unprecedented as a casting at that date. To cast many of the larger pieces, all three furnaces at the Holmes had to be run and tapped at the same time. When the centre arch was erected at the Holmes it attracted such crowds of sightseers that the local bakers had to work overtime to keep them fed. The Act for the bridge was passed in 1811 with construction starting in 1814 and finishing in 1819. Tolls paid for passage over were expected to meet the cost of the construction. Unfortunately the approaches to the bridge were awkward and the public preferred to walk a little further and cross free at London Bridge. In 1811, when they took the contract, the Walkers had taken shares to the value of £25,000 in the project. These proved largely worthless and they had the greatest difficulty in obtaining payments of their bills from the directors. In 1820 the journal reports that Samuel III and Joshua II had met the Southwark Bridge Committee and that their outstanding bill had been agreed at £31,925. The following year Joshua reported that there had been no alternative than to agree to the Bridge Company's offer of 10s in the pound on their debt.

In 1812 the capital of Joshua Walker and Co. was valued at £299,015 and that of Walkers and Booth at £55,556. The ironworks at Gospel Oaks, Tipton (Sts) was purchased in 1817 to support the Rotherham operations. Samuel Walker III moved to Staffordshire to superintend the works. Within three years, however, the partners were taking a very gloomy view of the company's prospects and they began the process of winding down their operations in south Yorkshire. The end of the Napoleonic Wars in 1815 saw a drastic fall in the demand for cannon and it is likely that their concentration on the castings for Southwark Bridge had allowed other companies to steal some of the Walkers' markets. In 1816 they were complaining about the general stagnation of trade and depreciation of all kinds of property. The partners' meeting in 1820 resolved: 'That it appears the iron concern has become, from local and other disadvantages, an unprofitable concern and likely, instead of paying even common interest, to be a losing concern. It was therefore agreed that the whole concern shall be wound up as soon as circumstances shall admit.'

10

The Eighteenth Century

On the death of Jane Bickerton, second wife of the 6th Duke of Norfolk, at the Holmes in 1693 the lordship of the two manors with the Howard estates in Kimberworth and Rotherham passed to her elder son George Howard, who died without issue in 1721. His next elder brother James having drowned in 1702, Rotherham and Kimberworth passed to Jane's third son Frederick Henry Howard, who died without issue in 1727. Under the terms of his will, the manors and estates passed to a distant relative, Francis Howard, 7th Baron Howard of Effingham, descended from Thomas Howard, 2nd Duke of Norfolk (d. 1524) through his second wife. The elder son of this second marriage was William Howard, created Lord High Admiral and Lord Howard of Effingham in 1554. Charles Howard, famous as Howard of Effingham, commander of the fleet at the defeat of the Armada, who was later created Earl of Nottingham, was William's elder son. On the death of the third Earl of Nottingham without heirs in 1681, the earldom ceased, but the title of Lord Howard of Effingham passed to the descendants of William Howard, the 1st Earl's younger brother.

George II created Francis Howard Deputy Earl Marshal of England and Earl of Effingham in 1731 'in consideration of his great merits and abilities'. His son Thomas, 2nd Earl, followed a military career and was Colonel of the 1st Troop of the Horse Grenadier Guards. On his death in 1763 his 16-year-old son, Thomas, succeeded him. Thomas obtained a commission as ensign in the Coldstream Guards at the age of 15, transferring to the 68th

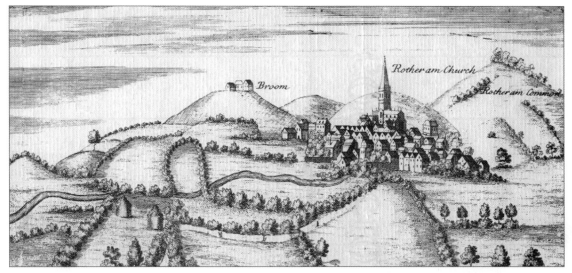

A view of Rotherham as seen from Car House *c.* 1740, showing the town clustered around the parish church. The isolated building to the right of the church is probably Moorgate Hall. (*Rotherham Central Library*)

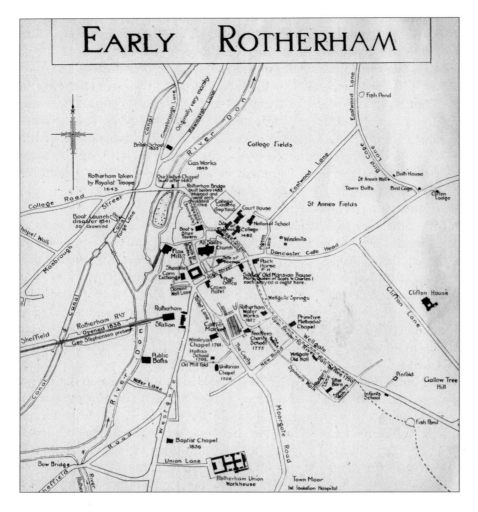

EARLY ROTHERHAM

Rotherham as it was in the 18th and early 19th centuries.

Foot as captain four years later. In 1769 he obtained permission to take service in Russia with Catherine the Great and saw action against the Turks. He was serving with the 22nd Foot in Ireland when the regiment was ordered to America to serve against the rebellious colonists. Effingham felt bound to resign his commission rather than serve against the colonists. On 18 May 1775 he addressed the House of Lords, declaring his belief that Parliament had no right to tax the American colonies. He retired to civilian life, residing at Holmes Hall when he was not in London on parliamentary business. Holmes Hall was a relatively modest house and even before the earl leased part of the estate to the Walkers it was in close proximity to the slitting mill and furnace. The earl decided to move a mile or so further north, purchasing the Thundercliffe Grange estate, demolishing the old Grange and engaging the Rotherham architect John Platt to design and build a new Thundercliffe Grange a short distance away. Work started in 1776 and the main building was completed in October 1783, by which time Holmes Hall had been sold to the Walkers. The Earl also built himself a hunting lodge on the south side of the Don Valley, calling it Boston Castle in honour of the Boston Tea Party. Here the earl's guests were entertained with wine and punch, but the serving of tea was absolutely forbidden.

Effingham was a supporter of the Marquess of Rockingham and an opponent of the government of Lord North. The resignation of Lord North in 1782, as a result of the reverses in America, led to the appointment of Rockingham as prime minister. Although Rockingham died within a few months of taking up the office, Effingham became treasurer of the household and in 1784 was appointed to the lucrative post of Master of the Royal Mint. He resigned the Mint and the position of Deputy Grand Master of Freemasons on his appointment as Governor of Jamaica. The earl's wife died in October 1791 on passage from Jamaica to New York and he died the following month. They were both buried in the cathedral at Spanish Town, Jamaica. He was succeeded by his brother Richard, 4th Earl and 10th Baron Howard of Effingham, who used Thundercliffe as a summer residence until his death in 1816.

The 3rd Earl took a close interest in the affairs of Rotherham, becoming a feoffee in 1778, together with his brother, the Hon. Richard Howard, and Earl Fitzwilliam. By the end of the century the trust was in need of revision as the provision that a new election should take place whenever the number of feoffees fell below six had been frequently ignored: it had become increasingly difficult to find twelve suitable candidates at any one time. In 1798 it was agreed that vacancies could be filled by election as they occurred. At the same time changes were made which restricted the franchise to those holding property with an annual value of £10 or more and freeholders with property with the annual value of £2 or more. This disenfranchised the many small freeholders and tenants in the town. Candidates for office were required to own property worth £20 a year.

The income from their endowments gave the feoffees a freedom not available to the parish officers, who were constrained by the need to levy rates to raise income. Their long tenure of office encouraged them to take a longer view and plan for the future. The feoffees opened the century by improving the recreational facilities in the town. In 1706 they paid the costs of digging and walling 'ye cold Bath' on the east side of Bird Cage Lane (now Eastwood Lane), opposite St Ann's Well. In 1721 Edward Blyth was paid to stud up bushes on the Moor to enable the racecourse to be enlarged. This would seem to predate the previously

Boston Castle, off Moorgate, erected by the Earl of Effingham as a monument to his support of the American colonists in their War of Independence. (*Rotherham Central Library*)

known first reference to racing in the town in 1727. In 1707 they paid for a load of coal for a bonfire to mark the union between England and Scotland and in 1760 the accession of George II was marked by bonfires at the Hood Cross, the head of Bridgegate, Millgate, the High Street and two in Westgate. Unfortunately no accounts survive of the jollifications that must have gone on around the bonfires. More details survive of the celebrations to mark the centenary of the Glorious Revolution in 1788. A ball was held, probably in the Town Hall, on 4 November when 110 tickets were sold at 5s each and an excellent cold collation was provided. On the following day the gentlemen of the town and neighbourhood were joined by 700 members of the local friendly societies and 400 Sunday school scholars, with a band, in procession to the parish church where the Rev. William Harrison preached an excellent sermon. Around 80 gentlemen sat down to dinner in the town hall, presided over by the Earl of Effingham. On 6 November 400 Sunday school scholars were entertained at the Town Hall, dining off plum pudding, apple pies and 'broken victuals', i.e. the previous day's leftovers.

The almshouse (Chapel on the Bridge) was re-roofed in lead in 1732 at a cost of £9. Extraordinary charitable payments included £1 for 40 horse loads of coal supplied to the poor after a great storm in 1715. Further storms in 1768, 1774 and 1776 caused them to distribute large quantities of coal and bread. All this charity work was additional to that done by the overseers of the poor. A more unusual expense was the £4 3s 6d paid for making and painting a book press (bookshelves) in the vestry for 'the Bookes Mrs. Mansell gave'. This was the Mansel Library, a collection of theological works given to the parish church by Frances Mansel, widow of the Rev. Edward Mansel, vicar of Ecclesfield (d. 1704) and daughter of George Westby of Guilthwaite. The library remained in the parish church until 1893 when it was presented to the public library. The remaining volumes are now in the safe keeping of the Archives & Local Studies Section of Rotherham Library.

The Grammar School remained a regular charge in the feoffees' accounts. In 1707 they agreed to reimburse the schoolmaster, Mr Withers, for the costs of repairing a house near the

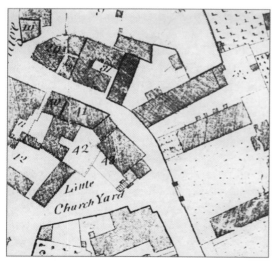

The new town hall of 1739, between College Street and the Little Churchyard, as shown on the 1774 plan of the town (building no. 43). (*Rotherham Central Library*)

school which became the official master's residence, at a cost to the feoffees of £75 4s 6d. The Grammar School finally found new premises in 1739 when the feoffees built a new town hall on Jesus Gate to replace the old building in the market-place. Between £500 and £600 was spent on the 'substantial and well-designed, if not handsome building' on a site extending from the old manorial bakehouse to the entrance to the Little Churchyard. Unfortunately no drawing or engraving of the building has survived but we do know that it was of two storeys with the main entrance on the first floor, reached by two flights of steps. The main hall was used for meetings of the Quarter Sessions, public balls and other events, 'the scene of the gayest and most hilarious assemblies in the district'. In 1775 the Earl of Effingham was given permission to hold his manor courts in the town hall upon payment of 6*d* a year. The Grammar School was accommodated on the ground floor and the feoffees held their own meetings in the town hall.

Although the Grammar School provided education for the better-off sons of the town there was little opportunity for the 'reclamation and culture of the neglected and otherwise untutored young of the impoverished working class'. The feoffees sought to remedy this by founding a Charity School in 1708 'for cloathing poor children and teaching them to read, write, knitt and sew, and for instructing them in the knowledge and duties of the Christian religion'. The Hon. Thomas Wentworth gave £136 to buy land for the benefit of the school and the Rev. Henry Robinson of St John's Church, Leeds, gave £100 for the same purpose. Numerous gentlemen gave smaller sums, amounting in all to £281

The Feoffees School on the Crofts, erected by John Platts for £276 11*s* 7*d* in 1775. (*Author*)

8*s* 9*d*. Mr Singleton was engaged as master at £12 a year and wool and oil (presumably lanolin) were purchased from Mr Downes to make the children's clothes. This was spun and made up by Mrs Cooper. A total of £2 15*s* 9½*d* was spent on 12 horn books, 30 spelling books, 15 New Testaments, 9 Bibles, 6 Books of Common Prayer, 19 catechism books, 24 paper (?exercise) books, 12 'accidences' (grammar books) and one of 'Dr Talbott's bookes'. In 1716 canvas and crewel wool was purchased to enable the girls to work samplers and Mrs Wood was engaged as mistress at £12 a year, less £2 for rent. The site of the original charity school is uncertain.

A manuscript set of rules to be observed by the scholars has survived, showing that the hours were 7 a.m. to 11 a.m. and 1 p.m. to 5 p.m. in summer, and 8 a.m. to 11 a.m. and 1 p.m. to 4 p.m. in winter. The pupils were also expected to report every Sunday and every Holy Day, to receive religious instruction. Holidays were three weeks at Christmas, a week at Easter, a week at Whitsun and two days at fair time. The master was to take special care to teach the children to read and spell well. When they could read, he could move on to teaching writing and arithmetic 'that they may be better qualified for Services and Apprenticeships'. The school was known as the Bluecoat School as the result of a decision taken in August 1775 that the boys' uniform was to be a blue jacket, breeches cut high on the hip and finished at mid-calf and blue caps with a small red front. The girls were to have blue serge dresses with narrow red cuffs, linen caps and tippets. In April 1775 the feoffees began to consult with John Platt about designing and building a new charity school on a site by the Beast Market. The cost was not to exceed £200. The job was given to John Platt who erected the building that still stands at the south-east corner of the Crofts, at a cost of £276 11*s* 7*d*. The design, with its broken three-bay pediment and round-topped arches, is typical of Platt's work and shows strong similarities with the stable block he designed for Samuel Walker at Masbrough Hall in 1768. The first master of the newly built school was Bartholomew Rotheram, who served until 1795 when John Clark, who served until 1831, replaced him.

John Platt had earlier been employed by the feoffees to alter Rotherham Bridge, adding a new 30 ft arch at the western end. The bridge was also widened to 24 ft 6 in by adding stonework to the upstream side. Platt had earlier, in 1764, rebuilt Bow Bridge over the Rother, near its confluence with the Don. Despite going over budget with the Charity School, the feoffees had no qualms in calling on John Platt again in 1778 to convert the Chapel on the Bridge into a gaol. The greaves were instructed to employ someone to examine the almshouse (Chapel on the Bridge) and report on the likely cost of converting it into a dwelling for the Deputy Constable with cells for the reception of prisoners. In February 1779 they contracted with Platt to alter the chapel into a prison at a cost not to exceed £36. Two cells were constructed in the crypt and the former almshouse at road level was converted into the constable's lodgings. The cells themselves have long gone but the cell doors, with their numerous carved names, remain in the crypt. As a result of the conversion Rotherham Bridge was given the alternative name of the Gaol Bridge, a name it retained long after the gaol had been transferred to the new court house in the 1820s. John Guest felt that the conversion of the almshouse into 'that repulsive receptacle of disorder and crime – a gaol' was 'a blot on the annals [of the feoffees] otherwise free from stain'.

Another building project started by the feoffees in 1779 was the erection of a market house in the market-place. They resolved to agree with Platt for the erection of a market house at a price not to exceed £156. In 1779 the price was raised to £168 to include the removal of the stocks and pillory. Elliott states that the building was never completed. Platt's own journal contains an enigmatic reference to the job under 9 August 1780: 'laid ye first

Rotherham Bridge showing the extra arch (left) and the stonework added in the 18th century to widen the roadway. (*Rotherham Central Library*)

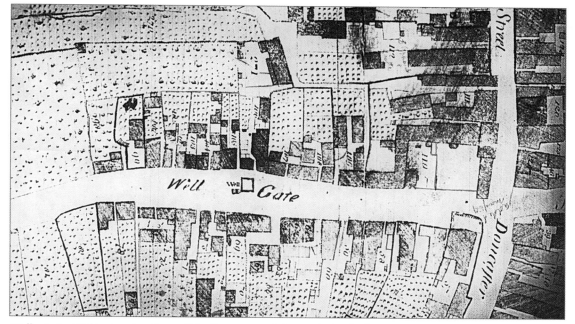

Wellgate in 1774, showing the well in the centre of the road. (*Rotherham Central Library*)

stone of the Market house at Rotherham. NB it was put a stop to, some time back.' The feoffees' accounts for 1781 contain an entry for the payment to Platt of £172 12s 6d for the market hall and £50 for paving the market-place. This would appear to be the full cost of the contract and it would be unlikely that the feoffees would have paid in full for something that had not been finished. The need to remove the stocks and pillory which stood in the centre of the market-place suggests that the market house was intended to occupy their place. In that case it would have been replaced by the corn exchange, built in 1841.

Throughout the century the feoffees were also concerned to maintain the town's water supply. The Wellgate spring provided 'a fine steam of beautiful limpid water', although it is unlikely that it was still limpid when it discharged into the Don near the Bridge. In 1709 nine labourers were paid 8s 7d for cleaning out the Wellgate brook and John Bower received 2s 2d for cleansing the large well in Wellgate. The stream was covered over from the bottom of the High Street in 1750. The Earl of Effingham's map of 1764 (Sheffield Archives, Arundel Castle Muniments, ACM Rot 104 – copy held by the Archives & Local Studies Section, Rotherham Library) shows the stream from the spring running down the centre of Wellgate into a rectangular cistern in the centre of the road. From there the overflow ran down the centre of the road before disappearing underground just short of the junction with High Street. The 1774 plan of the town shows the rectangular 'well' in the centre of the road and another well, Bishop's Well, in Wellgate, near Radley Row. In 1791–2 £285 11s was spent on the water supply from the wells. A number of cattle troughs were installed in Wellgate with a spout for the public supply. The overflow from the troughs was carried in an aqueduct above street level, with spouts at intervals, before it emptied itself into the covered drain along Jesus Gate and Bridgegate. The main public supply was a spout by the steps leading up to the town hall in Jesus Gate. The Domine Well was reputed to supply the purest water in town. The

Clifton House, probably designed by John Carr for Joshua Walker, was erected in 1783 and has housed the town's museum since 1893. (*Rotherham Central Library*)

inhabitants of Kimberworth had to rely on a variety of wells and streams for their water supply. Many inhabitants of Masbrough used the Don or the Holmes Tail Goit. This may sound unpalatable to those who know the state of the Don in recent years, but in 1890 William Creswick could remember taking trout of 2 lb out of the river between the Bridge Inn and the chapel and from the Holmes Tail Goit in the early years of the 19th century. The water at Masbrough was generally so bad that men could be seen queuing at 5 a.m. on Sundays to fill buckets at the Wellgate spring to take back to Masbrough.

The 18th century saw both an industrial and an agricultural revolution. Rotherham's contribution to the agricultural revolution was the Rotherham plough, designed *c*. 1729 by Joseph Foljambe of Eastwood. It was a lighter but mechanically more efficient design that could be pulled by only two horses. Foljambe assigned his design to Disney Staniforth of Firbeck who patented it in 1730. Although the patent was later set aside on the grounds that it was an improvement rather than a new design, the Rotherham plough had a profound effect on the design of ploughs throughout England and Scotland.

The second half of the 18th century saw a great change in the surroundings of Rotherham as the remaining common fields, commons and pastures were enclosed. The impetus for enclosure came from the local landowners, who saw the advantage of being able to consolidate their holdings into more manageable blocks on which they would be able to introduce the latest improvements in agricultural technique. The losers were the small tenants who lost their common rights and were left with small areas of land and the expense of fencing it. In parishes where one owner controlled all or almost all of the land, as with the Marquis of Rockingham at Greasbrough, he was able to enclose it at will without need of parliamentary sanction.

The earliest township within the parish to be enclosed was Rotherham itself, the Act being passed in 1762 and the award completed in 1764. The total area to be enclosed was estimated at 970 acres but the actual land enclosed was 1,034 acres. The Earl of Effingham as lord of the manor and lay rector was entitled to an allotment in lieu of his ownership of the great tithes. The small tithes belonged to the vicar and the Act shows that these had been commuted for annual money payments: 4d for every plough, foal, dovecote and malt kiln, 4d from every person engaged in trade, 2d for every house, 2d for each communicant, 1d for each hive of bees, ¼d in the shilling on servants' wages, 1d for each garden and 1½d for each milk cow. The main landholders were stated to be Thomas, Earl of Rotherham, William, Earl of Bessborough, and Catherine Buck, widow. The commissioners appointed a surveyor to ascertain the acreage of lands held by each proprietor. As with many early enclosure awards, the Rotherham award was purely written and was not accompanied by an official enclosure map. Luckily the Earl of Effingham decided that a map would be useful to him and employed George Kelk to draw up a map showing the various enclosures and roads that were awarded.

No sooner had the Rotherham enclosure been completed than work started on enclosing Masbrough under an Act of 1765. Here the remaining unenclosed land comprised common or waste ground known as Masbrough Common, the Clough, Masbrough Green, Walk Mill Moor and Pool Green, with common fields. In all there was 103 acres to be enclosed. Masbrough Common lay either side of Clough Road while Masbrough Green lay at the junction of Masbrough Street and Holmes Lane. In this case there was an enclosure map, by Sheffield surveyor William Fairbank, although strangely it dates from 1763, predating the Enclosure Act. The map shows a number of coal pits on Masbrough Common and the location of the school that Samuel Walker constructed at the Yellands.

Ferham House at Masbrough is another Walker house, constructed for Jonathan Walker by John Platt in 1761. It is now a nursing home.
(*Rotherham Central Library*)

The Buck family's town house on Bridgegate, now a furniture shop. (*Author*)

There was then a lull in proceedings before the passage of the act for the enclosure of Kimberworth in 1796. A plan of *c.* 1765 shows that the fields of Kimberworth were still divided into strips. By 1796, 424 acres of open fields, commons and waste remained unenclosed. The Earl of Effingham, as lord of the manor, received ⅟₇ of the commons and waste and a further ⅟₈ in lieu of the tithes of the commons and wastes. By the time the Enclosure Act for Brinsworth was passed in 1812, there only remained the meadow and pasture known as Bradmarsh and a few other parcels of commons or waste amounting to 220 acres.

When Arthur Young visited the Rotherham area in the 1760s as part of his investigations into agriculture and industry, he was particularly taken with the cabbages grown by Samuel Tooker on his land at Moorgate. These averaged 10 lb each with some reaching 20 lb or even 30 lb. Young gives a useful list of local prices at the time, including bread at 1½*d* a lb, butter 6*d* a lb, beef and mutton 3½*d* a lb and cheese 4*d* a lb. A 2-ton wagonload of coal could be bought for 10*s* 6*d*.

The industrial and agricultural prosperity of the town in the 18th century is shown by the number of fine houses that were erected in and around Rotherham. Samuel Walker built himself a house near his new works at Masbrough in 1749, replacing it with Masbrough Hall in 1768–9 (demolished in the 1860s). The stables, designed by John Platt, survived until the 1970s. Platt also designed Ferham House (now a nursing home), between Masbrough and Kimberworth, for Jonathan Walker II. John Carr of York may have designed Joshua Walker's house at Clifton, now Clifton Park Museum. Carr did design Eastwood House, on the Doncaster road, which was built for Joseph Walker in 1787 and demolished in the 1920s. A number of prominent families had houses in the town centre. The Buck family's house on Bridgegate survives as a furniture shop.

11

Church and Chapel

Religion in the 18th Century

The Toleration Act of 1689 allowed Dissenters to worship in their own meeting houses, licensed by the bishop, provided that their ministers subscribed to the Thirty-Nine Articles (except on baptism and church government). Catholics and Unitarians were excluded, however, and non-Anglicans continued to suffer civil disabilities under the Clarendon Code until the early 19th century.

In 1704 Rotherham's oldest congregation, the Presbyterians or Unitarians, gained their own meeting house through the generosity of Thomas Hollis (1634–1718). The son of a Rotherham whitesmith, Hollis moved to London after completing his apprenticeship as a cutler. He subscribed to the erection of Sheffield's first nonconformist chapel on Snig Hill and, in 1700, to its replacement, the Upper Chapel. The chapel in Rotherham dates to a

The original 1704 Unitarian Chapel on Downs Row, facing on to Oil Mill Fold. The new Hollis School was erected opposite the steps in 1879. (*Rotherham Central Library*)

The Hollis School at the top of Oil Mill Fold, erected in 1789. The upper storey was added in 1866. When the school was demolished the inscribed stone over the door was fixed to the chapel wall. (*Rotherham Central Library*)

deed of 1704 by which David Gass conveyed to Thomas Hollis junr and nine others the upper end of a croft near the Beast Market upon which it was intended to erect a meeting house. The site was to revert to Thomas Hollis senr and his heirs if it ceased to be used for worship. This reversion to the elder Hollis suggests that the impetus for the building had come from him, but at the age of 70 he preferred his son to take the active part in the trust.

The meeting house stood at the end of Downs Row, leading off Moorgate Street. The school for the education of poor children attached to the meeting house had a slightly earlier origin in an endowment made by Thomas Hollis senr in 1702, paying the master £20 a year for teaching between 23 and 30 children. The school seems to have been held in the chapel until a new school was erected in 1789. Thomas Hollis senr also purchased a house for the minister on Westgate. The original chapel could hold about 150 worshippers, with the usual congregation of about 100. The main entrance faced Westgate, with a side door giving access from Downs Row.

In 1789 Hollis School was rebuilt at the top of Oil Mill Fold. The sum of £399 6s was raised by subscription, including £155 from Timothy Hollis of London (grandson of Thomas Hollis senr), against a total cost of £481 10s 7d. The new school stood at the bottom of a flight of steps leading down from the meeting house. A second storey was added in 1866. The first master of the new school was Joseph Ramsbottom and among his early pupils was the young Ebenezer Elliott, of whom more anon. The rules of the school allowed children to attend for three years only and to be excluded if they were absent without due cause for more than 13 days in a quarter. They were to wear 'as decent apparel as the circumstances of their parents will admit'. Scholars were expected to attend the Sunday school and public worship every Sunday, both morning and afternoon, and were not to be absent for more than three Sundays, upon pain of exclusion. The control of the master and minister extended outside school hours, and any pupil found guilty of profane swearing, lying, pilfering or playing in the streets or fields on a Lord's Day would be punished.

The final 18th-century minister at Downs Row was Dr Thomas Warwick who combined his ministry with the practice of medicine and the pursuit of chemical investigations. He was accustomed to lecture on physiology in the meeting house on Sunday afternoons and started a book society at the school 'founded on liberal principles'. In 1801 he went into partnership with his brother-in-law, John Aldred, in a chemical works on a site next to Wellgate House, manufacturing wood acid which was used to form acetates of iron, lime and copper for use as mordants in dying and as dye for calico printing. Dr Warwick devised a Turkey red dye that was popular with the Manchester cotton printers. He was also the first person to develop a fast yellow dye. When the business failed in 1816 he left Rotherham, spending a short time as minister at Dukinfield (Chs) and devoting the rest of his life to scientific experimentation.

After the construction of the Downs Row meeting house in 1704, it was to be more than half a century before Rotherham had another permanent nonconformist meeting house. The first visit of John Wesley (1703–91) to the Rotherham area was in 1733 when he accompanied his father, the Rev. Samuel Wesley, Rector of Epworth (Lin), to consult the library at Wentworth Woodhouse. While at Oxford in 1729 Wesley had been a member of a group of devout Christians, who were known as the Methodists because they advocated strictly following the method of study and practice laid down in church statutes. When the churches were shut against him he held meetings in fields and organised local religious societies. Thorpe Hesley became the cradle of Methodism in the Rotherham area in 1738 when Samuel Birks invited the preacher David Taylor to come from Sheffield to preach. Among the early adherents of the church was the Thorpe schoolmaster William Green. Drawn by news of David Taylor's preaching, Wesley came to Sheffield for the first time in 1742 and afterwards paid the first of many visits to Barley Hall, where he preached twice. The preachers frequently had to run the gauntlet of the local mob that bitterly resented their doctrines and preaching. In 1744 Charles

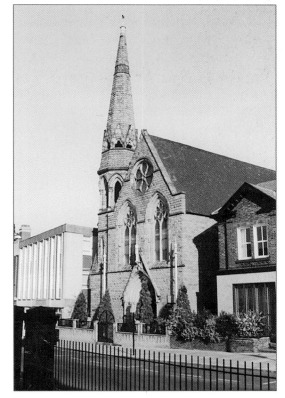

The Church of Our Father, Moorgate, was erected in 1879 to replace the chapel on Downs Row. The building is now a mosque. (*Author*)

Wesley, brother of John, together with Samuel Birks senr were ambushed in the centre of Thorpe Hesley. Luckily the 18-year-old Samuel Birks was returning from ploughing and rescued the party by driving his plough team through the mob. William Green moved to Rotherham in the 1740s and established a school whose pupils included the children of Samuel Walker. Green's school was well patronised by the middle classes who, while they did not share his religious beliefs, recognised him as an excellent teacher. The violent opposition to his teaching came from the working class, 'who had neither the disposition nor ability to give their children a proper education'. One of the most ardent opponents of the new doctrine was John Taylor who was wont to imitate the preaching of the Methodists in the local alehouses. One evening, opening the Bible to begin his satirical discourse, his eyes lighted on the verse 'Except ye repent, ye shall all likewise perish' (Luke, 3). This had such a profound effect on him that his satire turned into a true sermon and he became a staunch Methodist.

When Green first moved to Rotherham, he could only count on two or three poor people in Rotherham and two men and their wives in Masbrough as Methodists. The anti-Methodist mob in Rotherham could be quite as violent as that in Thorpe. One opponent, a butcher named Smith, would bodily carry the preacher away, and on another occasion drenched the unfortunate minister with a bucket of blood. By 1750 a proper Methodist class meeting was established in Rotherham and John Wesley became a regular visitor. Even the Marquis of Rockingham and his wife attended the preaching at Barley Hall on occasion. Wesley's first visit to Rotherham itself seems to have been in the summer of 1752 when he preached under a tree at Barley Hall and then in the evening in the open in Rotherham.

John Wesley preached here. Talbot Lane Methodist Church occupies the site of the Octagon Chapel, its 18th-century predecessor. (*Author*)

In 1757 the Rev. John Thorpe led a breakaway group, and with the support of Samuel and Aaron Walker and other followers of the modified Calvinism of George Whitfield, established an Independent congregation at Masbrough. In 1760 William Green was able to strengthen his own position by obtaining a licence to preach from the Archbishop of York. The following year the Rotherham Methodists saw the erection of a permanent meeting house on Bunting Croft, to the west of the cattle market in the Crofts. Wesley believed that the octagon was the perfect plan for a Methodist meeting house and this design was adopted in Rotherham. Green wrote to Wesley to entreat him to come and preach in the new building, and in July 1761 Wesley preached in the uncompleted shell, recording in his journal that 'the congregation was larger than ever, the Society well united, and much alive to God'. William Green seems to have borne the cost of the building, which amounted to some £270.

Masbrough Independent Chapel was rebuilt in 1777. The 19th-century additions can be seen at the right. The original chapel is now used as a carpet warehouse. (*Author*)

In 1771 the chapel trustees gave Green a 999-year lease of part of the chapel yard so that he could build a school there, in recompense for the 'great expense, trouble, and loss of time' that he had been put to in erecting the chapel. Wesley preached in the completed chapel in March 1764, recording on that occasion that on his second day preaching 'an ass walked gravely in at the gate, came up to the door of the house, lifted up his head and stood stock still in a posture of deep attention'.

During Wesley's lifetime there had been no open breach with the Anglican Church, but after his death in 1791 Methodism became a separate denomination with its own chapels. Membership of the Rotherham circuit stood at 820 in 1797 but had fallen to 498 in 1800. The first register of membership included 123 members in Rotherham, 32 at Masbrough, 5 at Bradgate, 15 at Greasbrough, 6 at Scholes and 43 at Thorpe Hesley. Despite their decline in numbers, the Rotherham members decided that the Octagon Chapel no longer suited their purposes and decided on a larger building. The Octagon Chapel and William Green's school were demolished and a larger chapel on a more conventional plan, preachers' houses and stables were erected in 1807. The cost was £2,500, half being raised by subscriptions and the remainder borrowed at interest.

The Methodists who followed John Thorpe and the Walkers when they split from the main body met initially in a schoolroom at Masbrough, possibly the school built by Samuel Walker at the Yellands in 1756. A few years later the Walkers built a chapel on Back Lane (now College Road) close to the site where Samuel was to erect Masbrough Hall in 1768–9. In 1762 the Walker journal relates: 'and this year the Meeting House was built so far as to

The roof of the Walker Mausoleum, erected by Samuel Walker between Masbrough Hall and Masbrough Independent Chapel, peeks above the foliage that threatens to engulf it. (*Author*)

be covered in'. The Rev. Mr Edwards from Leeds opened the chapel on 1 January 1764. There were then sixteen members with the Rev. Mr Thorpe as minister and Samuel Walker and Benjamin Longley as deacons. The chapel served until 1777 when it was pulled down and replaced by a new structure on the same site. Again the bulk of the expense was born by Samuel Walker, assisted by a bequest of £300 from his brother Aaron. It is this building that still stands on College Road, now used as a carpet warehouse. The new chapel was finished in 1778 but was not licensed until 1780, by which time the congregation numbered some 45 members.

Samuel Walker erected a family mausoleum between Masbrough Hall and the chapel yard, which has been dated to the early 19th century. The Walker journal, however, refers to the building of 'a vault or burying ground' in 1776 and it is clearly shown on a map of 1803, so the present building may be a later remodelling of an earlier structure. Although the entrance is from the chapel burial ground, the mausoleum was never part of the chapel property, and although now under the care of Rotherham Metropolitan Borough Council it is still, in theory, owned by the surviving members of the Walker family.

The Attercliffe Academy run by the Rev. Timothy Jollie was noted for educating numbers of Dissenting ministers in the late 17th and early 18th centuries. Writing in May 1700, Oliver Heywood recorded that Jollie then had 26 pupils at Attercliffe and 'forty more completely qualified and now employed in the sacred office'. After Jollie's death the Rev. John Wadsworth, formerly minister at Rotherham, succeeded him. He was not a success as tutor and the academy closed before his death in 1745. Thereafter support for training

Independent ministers in Yorkshire relied on the Northern Education Society of London, supporting academies at Heckmondwike and later at Northowram. In 1794 the society informed Joshua Walker at Masbrough that they were withdrawing and the Yorkshire churches would have to take on the responsibility. A series of meetings in 1794 and 1795 culminated in the decision to found a college at Rotherham. Joshua Walker agreed to be responsible for erecting the college buildings on a site on the north side of Back Lane, Masbrough, a short distance from the Independent chapel. The college was a three-storey building, 46 ft by 28 ft with a hall and library on the ground floor. The upper floors each contained four lodging rooms and seven studies. The first tutor was Dr Edward Williams, recently appointed minister at Masbrough Independent chapel, who continued in both offices until his death in 1813, by which time about 50 ministers had graduated from the college.

A small Baptist congregation, numbering 21 members in 1791, began to meet at Clough Road, Masbrough, in 1789 and moved to a new meeting house at the south end of Westgate in 1837. The burial ground beside the Clough Road meeting house remained in use after the move.

Despite the growth of nonconformity in its varied forms during the 18th century, the parish church remained the main place of worship in the town throughout the century. Even the Dissenters were forced to use the services of the vicar when they wished to be married, and many were buried in the churchyard as the chapels and meeting house had only small burial grounds or none at all.

During the 18th century the bell ringers continued to turn out to celebrate each and every national success, mostly English victories in the wars of William III and Anne and the defeat of the Jacobites in 1715. The great tenor bell cracked in 1704 and had to be replaced at a cost of £50 12s 11½d including carriage by water as far as Doncaster. It was the custom that the township of Rotherham paid one half of the costs of the upkeep of the church, while the other townships (Tinsley, Brinsworth, Greasbrough and Kimberworth) shared the other half. By the middle of the century the box pews, inserted piecemeal by individual parishioners, were an increasing inconvenience. In 1743 a faculty was obtained to move the pulpit and font to more suitable positions and to take down and rebuild the lofts or galleries and the pews in the nave 'which at present greatly obstruct the voice of the Officiating Minister'. Three years later a licence was issued to allow the new seating to be assigned to parishioners. The largest pew, across the aisle from the pulpit, was assigned to the Earl of Effingham and contained ten seats. It is possible that nothing was done about the galleries under this faculty as a further faculty was issued in 1760. This gave power to take down the gallery at the east end, known as the scholars' loft, and to erect galleries to the south, north and west of the church, to be 16 ft 6 in wide, 10 ft 7 in high at the front and 14 ft at the back, plastered underneath to prevent dust falling on worshippers below. Sixteen years later permission was obtained to insert an organ loft in the eastern arch of the tower with galleries within the north and south arches in the tower crossing. A new organ by the celebrated maker Johan Snetzler was installed in the organ loft. The pew rents from the new galleries were used to pay the salary of the organist. In 1763 Samuel Jenkinson of Whiston was paid £11 2s 0d for whitewashing the interior of the church (2,674 sq yd at 1d per yard). In 1777 he did the same job in 27 days for only £7 12s 6d.

In 1792 a strip of the churchyard was given up to allow Ratten Row to be widened. The churchyard was enlarged in 1794 by the purchase, from the Earl of Effingham, and

The memorial to Samuel Buck of Rotherham (d. 1806) by the sculptor Flaxman. This memorial is now in the south transept of the parish church. (*Rotherham Central Library*)

demolition of the house adjoining the vicarage, at the top of Vicarage Lane, at a cost of £438. The old Ring O'Bells can be dated by the resolution of a town meeting in 1796 that Ratten Row should be widened from Mr Watson's house to the Church Steps and that Mr Buck be prevailed on to build the new inn partly on the churchyard to fall in line with the widening.

The death of the vicar, the Rev. William Harrison, in 1794, led to a dispute over his successor. The Rev. George Smith had been appointed as a curate in Sheffield parish church in 1789 and had also undertaken the tutorship of the son of Jonathan Walker of Ferham. On the death of Mr Harrison, Smith, on the recommendation of Jonathan Walker, obtained a promise of the living from the Earl of Effingham. There was a faction in the town that preferred the candidature of the Rev. Richard Burton, curate in the parish church and master of the grammar school. His supporters denounced Smith as a supporter of Jacobinism (i.e. a radical) and an associate of dissenting preachers. A petition to that effect received 400 signatures in two hours. Although Smith defended himself against the charges, the earl eventually decided that Smith was not a fit candidate, and appointed the Rev. George Bayliffe, son of one of the assistant ministers at Sheffield parish church.

12

The Nineteenth Century

With the opening of the 19th century the town began to take steps to regulate its own affairs, starting with an Act of Parliament to enable the market-place to be improved. Passed in June 1801, the *Act for enlarging and improving the Market Place . . . of Rotherham* established a Company of Proprietors empowered to raise £4,150, divided into £50 shares, to enable them to enlarge the market-place, improve the approaches and erect proper slaughterhouses. The proprietors' first act was to sweep away the old Shambles, between the market-place and Church Street. In its place a new, single-storey stone Shambles was erected, consisting of 28 shops on the exterior with 20 butchers' and fishmongers' stalls around the interior courtyard. Proper slaughterhouses were erected on the riverbank, to the west of the market, and in 1841 a corn exchange and butter market was opened in the centre of the market-place.

The 1801 Market Act also enacted that every owner or occupier of property worth £20 p.a. was appointed a commissioner for cleansing, lighting and regulating the streets. The commissioners introduced street lighting to the town centre, installing a number of oil lamps. In the interests of economy, they were only lit during the winter months and then not when there was a full moon. A stone column that carried one of these oil lamps can still be seen on a wall in Wellgate.

In other areas private enterprise began to fill the vacuum caused by a lack of true local government. A private water company was formed in 1827, installing a steam engine on Quarry Hill, above Wellgate, and pumping water from the Wellgate spring to a reservoir in the Crofts. From here water was piped to householders who were prepared to pay for the privilege of a supply. This supply was, however, never sufficient to meet demand and often only ran for an hour or two each day. The Rotherham Gas Light and Coke Company was formed in 1833 to erect a gas works on the riverbank just to the north of Rotherham Bridge.

The interior of the Shambles showing some of the butchers' stalls. This photograph was taken in about 1905, shortly before demolition. (*Rotherham Central Library*)

The Walkers' decision to wind down their Rotherham operations could have been a disaster for the town, given their dominant position in local industry. Luckily they decided on an orderly closure phased over several years and most of their sites remained in production under new owners, often former Walker workmen. The works at the Holmes were initially sold to the Don Navigation, who wished to control the abstraction of water. In 1829 the site was leased to Matthew Habershon. Under his son, Joseph Jones Habershon, the company specialised in cold-rolled steel sheet for pen nibs and crinoline frames. The Holmes blast furnaces were taken over by Geach and Co. of Parkgate (later Park Gate Iron and Steel Co.) and remained in production until the 1920s. Part of the works at Masbrough were taken over by Warrington toolmakers Peter Stubs and Co., who were looking for a site to manufacture their own high-grade steel. In 1842 they purchased Holmes Hall. The hall was demolished to erect the Warrington Works, comprising both cementation furnaces and crucible furnaces.

The New Foundry on Rawmarsh Road was started by Clay and Co., in competition with the Walkers, and then sold to Ebenezer Elliott senr, a former clerk of the Walkers. It was in the house at the Foundry that Ebenezer Elliott junr, Rotherham's foremost literary figure of the 19th century, was born in 1781. The elder Elliott belonged to an austere Calvinist sect and is said to have baptised his own son in the canal. Despite minimal formal education, Ebenezer junr became famous as the 'Corn Law Rhymer', penning many poems against the iniquities of the Corn Laws, introduced in 1815 to keep the price of English corn high

The west end of the market-place, showing the Royal Oak and the rear of the Corn Exchange (left). All this property was demolished when the Market Hall was built in 1878–9. (*Rotherham Central Library*)

and to prevent the import of cheaper foreign grain. He took over the foundry after his father's death, but proved a better poet than a businessman and went bankrupt *c.* 1819. He then moved to Sheffield where he set up a wholesale iron and steel business and agency for the Walkers' Gospel Oaks works. In later life he retired to Hargate Hill, near Darfield, where he died in 1849, the year of the final repeal of the Corn Laws.

James Yates, a relative and ex-employee of the Walkers, took over their foundry interests in partnership with Charles Sandford. Sandford and Yates also took over the New Foundry, later renamed the Phoenix Works, and also, in 1831, the Rotherham Foundry on Domine Lane. When the two partners split in 1838 Sandford, with William Owen, retained the Phoenix Works, specialising in the production of railway wheels and axles. Yates retained the foundry business and took over the former Masbrough Flax Works, manufacturing a wide range of stove grates, cooking ranges and other cast-iron goods. The company, later Yates, Haywood and Co.,

The surviving oil lamp column in Wellgate. (*Author*)

built a large new factory, Effingham Works, on Thames Street, Masbrough, in 1855, reputedly then the largest of its kind in Europe. During the 19th century Rotherham became an important centre of the stove grate industry, with companies such as George Wright and Co., Micklethwaite and Skelton, Corbitt and Co. producing large quantities of cast-iron goods of all descriptions. The early success of Sandford and Owen, later Owens Patent Wheel, Tire and Axle Co. Ltd., in mass producing wheels and axles for the infant railway system led to the town becoming a centre for the production of railway wheels. Coal, for which the 19th century had an insatiable desire, was moved around the railway system in thousands of wagons. These wagons ran on wheels and axles that were produced by Rotherham companies such as Harrison and Camm, at the Holmes (where they also made complete wagons), John Baker and Co. at the Brinsworth Iron and Wheel Works at New York, Masbrough, and Owen and Dyson on Fullerton Road, Ickles. Many of the wagons run by colliery companies were hired from companies such as the North Central Wagon Co. of Rotherham.

Brass founding became another Rotherham speciality. This originated with the Chrimes family who were plumbers and glaziers in the town at the turn of the century. Edward Chrimes patented the modern, screw-down tap in 1845. On Edward's death in 1847 his brother Richard returned from London to take over the company, and went into partnership with John Guest. The spread of piped water supplies in towns, coupled with the use of gas for lighting, enabled Guest and Chrimes to build up an extensive business supplying taps and valves of all sizes, fire hydrants and water and gas meters. The

The Thames Street frontage of Yates and Haywood's Effingham Works, erected in 1855. (*Author*)

brassworks was initially on the riverbank, below the market-place, but this site soon became too cramped. In 1857 a new factory was erected on Don Street, on the other side of the river. Other brassworks, such as Gummers (1871) and William Baines and Co., opened in the town later in the century.

Another industry that still exists in the town is the production of glass bottles. The first glass cone was erected adjoining the Don Navigation at Masbrough in 1751. In 1783 John Beatson of Bentley Grange (WYk) purchased the works for his son William. The present company, Beatson Clark and Co. Ltd, resulted from the marriage of Ann Beatson and John Graves Clark in 1827. By the middle of the century there were three glass cones in production, turning out bottles of all shapes and sizes.

One forgotten 19th-century Rotherham industry is the production of linen thread. Tenter Street at Masbrough takes its name from Tenter Meadow where the linen cloth was stretched out to bleach in the sun. It is a reminder of the Masbrough Flax Mill, run by William Beatson in parallel with the glassworks and converted into a foundry by James Yates. In 1835–6 the town corn mill, converted into a rolling mill by the Walkers, was rebuilt by Thomas Johnson of Doncaster, as a flax mill. The mill was a major provider of female employment, at between 5s and 16s for a 12-hour week, and its closure in the 1860s was a major blow to the town.

The foundation of Rotherham as a major steel-producing town was laid by the establishment of the Phoenix Bessemer Steel Works at the Ickles in 1871. Although this enterprise failed in 1875, Henry Steel purchased the assets under the title Steel, Tozer and Hampton. When Thomas Hampton left the board in 1883 William Henry Peech replaced him. As Steel, Peech and Tozer the company became a major force in the English steel industry. The original works at the Ickles were expanded greatly with the addition of cogging and rail mills and plant for manufacturing springs and railway axles. By 1897 the original Bessemer converters had been replaced by three open-hearth furnaces.

In 1850 it was estimated that there were 365 persons in the town employed in casting and forging, 350 in the stove grateworks, 70 in rolling mills and tilt hammers, 65 in iron and steelmaking, 50 at nailmaking, 30 in the glassworks, 35 in potteries, 70 in brassworks, 47 in chemical works, 82 in breweries and 100+ in collieries. In addition 200 of the *c.* 600 men employed at the Parkgate ironworks lived in Rotherham or Masbrough.

The spread of industry led to a great increase in the market for coal, both locally and nationally. The small, shallow pits of the 18th century were replaced with deep mines, using steam engines both for pumping water out and for raising and lowering coal and men. The

Guest and Chrimes' factory on Don Street to which the company moved in 1857. (*Author*)

growth in the industrial workforce led to increasing demand for housing. In 1801 the population of Rotherham township was 3,070 and of Kimberworth 3,326. Ten years later the Rotherham figure had fallen to 2,950 but Kimberworth had risen to 3,482 and in 1841 the respective figures were 5,505 and 5,066. By 1851 the population of the parish had risen to 16,822. The next decade saw a big rise, to 24,098, of whom 13,547 lived in Kimberworth, Masbrough and Greasbrough and 8,390 in Rotherham. In 1901 the population had climbed to 61,541, with 24,558 in Rotherham township and 30,581 in Kimberworth, Masbrough and Greasbrough. The remaining 6,402 were divided between the outer townships of Brinsworth, Catcliffe, Orgreave and Dalton. In 1850 there were reckoned to be 2,261 houses in Rotherham and Kimberworth.

The demand for accommodation led to the construction of houses on every available piece of land in Rotherham and Masbrough. Even in the town centre the once elegant gardens sprouted rows of two up, two down or back-to-back houses. Their names, for example, Garden Row and True Briton Yard, belied the condition in which their inhabitants lived with no running water and inadequate sanitation. With no proper sewers or drains, infectious diseases spread rapidly in the courts and yards, and the mortality rate was high, reaching 1 in 37 by 1850. Fever, diarrhoea and dysentery were endemic in the poorer parts of the town. When cholera broke out in 1832, the eight surgeons in the town were able to do little to halt its spread and 31 died; the first nine were buried in the churchyard but subsequent burials were in the cholera burial ground at East Dene (now surrounded by the council houses on Park Road). There was no hospital in Rotherham. A public dispensary, supported by public subscriptions, was started in a building on Wellgate in 1806 to provide medical assistance to those living within a mile of the parish church. It was moved to a new building, on the site of the 18th-century town hall, in College Street, in 1828. There was no provision for in-patients and the seriously ill had to be taken to the infirmary in Sheffield.

Matters were so bad that in 1850 a petition was sent to the Government calling for a public enquiry under the Public Health Act. This duly took place in the court house during August, and the inspector, William Lee, had little trouble finding witnesses to come forward with tales of cellars flooded by foul water, wells filling with sewage and foul excretions oozing through house walls. There was also much evidence about the inadequacy of the water supply. The water company was only able to supply 50 per cent of the town, and often for only two or three hours a day in summer. People living at Kimberworth had to rise at 2 a.m. or 3 a.m. to be sure of getting water from the local wells. Lee recommended that a local board of health, consisting of 12 members, be established for Rotherham and Kimberworth with a view to establishing a proper, constant supply of clean water, proper sewerage and drainage. The powers of the board with regard to main sewerage were also to extend to Brinsworth.

Moulders at Guest and Chrimes, photographed outside their workshop in the 1870s. (*Rotherham Central Library*)

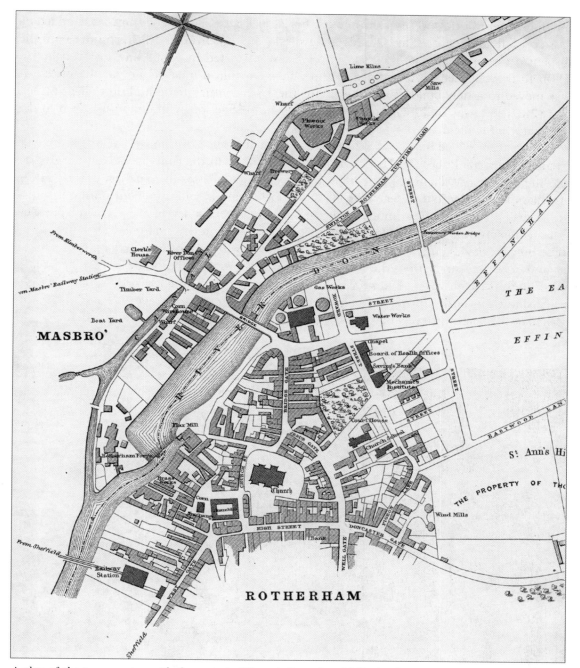

A plan of the town centre, with the main buildings indicated, *c.* 1860. (*Rotherham Central Library*)

Once constituted, the Board of Health set to work to improve the town, digging up the streets to lay sewers and drains. The water company was taken over in 1853 and over the next two years powerful pumping engines were erected on College Fields (the site of the present entrance to the bus station on Frederick Street) with reservoirs at Boston Castle and at Kimberworth to enable the whole town to benefit from piped water. In 1863 powers were

Two of the surviving cholera gravestones in the churchyard. (*Author*)

The building of the Rotherham Dispensary on College Street was erected in 1828. To the right, on the corner, are the premises occupied by the Grammar School between 1828 and 1857. At the left the Assembly Rooms can be seen against the churchyard wall. (*Rotherham Central Library*)

obtained to increase the supply by taking water from the Pinch Mill Spring near Whiston and from streams at Dalton. The gas company was also taken over and in 1868 the local board was able to acquire all the shares in the market company.

The year 1850 was also an important milestone for the development of the town, as it was then that the Earl of Effingham obtained a private Act of Parliament enabling him to break an entail in a family settlement that prevented him from granting leases for more than 21 years. The earl began to develop his land to the north of College Street and Bridgegate, laying out Effingham Street, Howard Street, and Frederick Street, and leasing plots for building. One of the first buildings to be erected was the offices for the Local Board of Health on Howard Street, the embryo of the later town hall. Also in the middle of the century Eastwood Hall and the Eastwood Estate were purchased by Benjamin Badger and T.S. Badger Eastwood. They laid out roads (Fitzwilliam Road, Cottenham Road, etc.) and divided the estate into building plots.

One other result of the 1850 public enquiry was the closure of the churchyard to further burials in 1854. The area of the churchyard was completely inadequate for a parish the size of Rotherham and grave spaces had to be reused every nine years. However, a private cemetery had been established off Moorgate in 1841. This was originally unconsecrated and was used only for nonconformist burials, but a consecrated section was added in 1846. The proprietors sold the cemetery to the burial board in 1855 for £2,500.

The growth of industry and population was paralleled by improvements in communications. The Don Navigation, extended to Sheffield by the Sheffield Canal of 1819, remained an important means of transport throughout the century, although it was faced by increased competition from the growing railway network. In 1835 a new cut was made from Rotherham to Jordan, bypassing the Bromley Sands and Jordan Cuts. The town was hit by tragedy in 1841 when a new barge, being launched from a dry dock off Masbrough Street, overturned. Many spectators had climbed on the barge to witness the launch and 50 were drowned, many of them children. The first public railway in the town, the Sheffield and Rotherham Railway, ran along the Don Valley from the Wicker, Sheffield, to Westgate, and opened in 1838. Construction of this line proceeded in parallel with the building of the North Midland Railway from Derby along the Rother Valley to Masbrough and to Leeds, which opened in 1840. Both lines later became part of the Midland Railway. The year 1847 saw both the Don Navigation, and its feeder the Dearne and Dove Canal, absorbed by the South Yorkshire Railway, which itself became part of the Manchester, Sheffield and Lincolnshire Railway. When the MSLR began construction of its Sheffield to Doncaster line via Rotherham, it utilised the line of the old cuts at Ickles and Bromley Sands and part of the 1835 cut to Rotherham. A new cut was made from the Don, near Westgate, to join the Holmes Cut. The MSLR was opened to Rotherham in 1868, when Main Street was constructed to connect the central station with the town centre. The line was extended to Mexborough in 1871.

At the beginning of the century, educational provision was limited to the Grammar School, the feoffees' and the Hollis schools, and a number of private schools and academies. A nonconformist British School was erected in Rawmarsh Road, Masbrough, in 1833 and the Methodists built a day school on Wilfred Street in 1860. When the town hall on College Street was demolished in 1827, new premises for the Grammar School, shared with the subscription library (founded 1775), were erected next to the new dispensary. The school remained here until 1857 when a new grammar school was built on Moorgate Road, comprising a large schoolroom and adjoining house for the master. National schools, run by the Anglican Church, were erected on College Lane in the town centre, and at Kimberworth (1830), Masbrough (1864), Eastwood (1870) and Thorpe Hesley. Even with these additional schools, there were insufficient places for all the children in the town even if their parents had been able to afford the fees. The Education Act of 1870 was intended to establish a national system of elementary education overseen by local school boards. It was not until 1875 that the Rotherham United District School Board, covering Rotherham, Kimberworth and Brinsworth, held its first meeting. The first schools opened by the board were at Thornhill and Wellgate

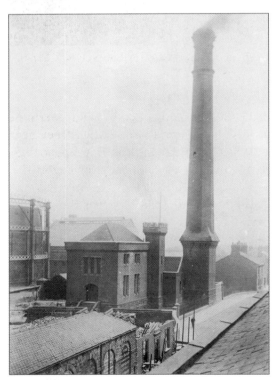

The waterworks pumping station, erected by the Local Board of Health on Frederick Street in 1855, with the gasworks behind. (*Rotherham Central Library*)

The town centre in the late 19th century, looking up High Street from Doncaster Gate. (*Rotherham Central Library*)

in 1879, followed by Blackburn and Kimberworth (1880), St Ann's Road (1893), Ferham Road (1894), Alma Road and Scholes (1896) and Doncaster Road, Park Street and Brinsworth in 1901. The board also took over the Feoffees' School and the Hollis School as temporary board schools, but both were closed when sufficient places were available in the board schools.

In the early 19th century, when many people could not afford a clock, it was the custom to ring one of the bells in the parish church at 5 a.m., 12 noon and 8 p.m. in summer and at 6 a.m., 12 noon and 6 p.m. in winter. Matthew Jessop was paid £9 9s a year for ringing the 'Hour Bell' in 1802. In 1820 the tenor bell fractured again and it was decided to hang a new peal of ten bells in the tower. The new peal cost, with fittings, £1,241 2s 8d with £539 17s allowed for the value of the old bells. The remaining cost was raised by public subscription and the new peal was inaugurated at Easter 1822. In October 1827 the vestry gave notice that it would no longer permit the statutes fair to be held in the churchyard and men would be employed to keep it clear on the day. The organ was taken from the loft in the tower in 1843 and placed in the north transept. In the 1840s a new vicarage was built on Moorgate and the old vicarage on the churchyard was used for a time as a temperance institute. By the time that the Rev. William Newton became vicar in 1873, it was clear that the church was in need of considerable restoration. A restoration committee was formed, which invited the noted architect Sir Gilbert Scott to carry out the

Alma Road School, a typical Board School, erected in 1896. (*Rotherham Central Library*)

work. He removed the galleries from the nave, cleaned and restored the stonework, repaired the north transept roof and replaced all the pews in the nave. The church was reopened, amid general rejoicing, in April 1875.

As the century progressed and the population of the town increased, it became increasingly difficult for the parish church to minister to a parish the size of Rotherham. There was also resistance from the outlying townships towards the payment of the church rate to the parish church: in 1850 the churchwardens of Greasbrough were refusing to pay their share of the rate and two years later the Tinsley share was well overdue. The Tinsley Chapel had been independent in all but name for many years but the exact date of its formal severance from Rotherham is unclear. In other areas new churches were erected, initially as chapels of ease, but later as parish churches in their own right – Thorpe Hesley (1839), Kimberworth (1843), Masbrough, St John (1864) and St Paul (1905), Eastwood, St Stephen (1874) and St Saviour (1901), Clifton, St James (1887), Northfield, St Michael (1870) and Brinsworth, St Andrew (1885) and St George (1898).

There was also a growth in the number of nonconformist chapels, partly to serve the growing population, but also as a result of splits in existing churches. A Primitive Methodist chapel was erected in Wellgate in 1851, replaced by a new chapel next door (now the masonic hall) in 1893. The Wesleyan Reform congregation built a Zion chapel next to the local board offices in Howard Street in 1853. This was soon too small and a new chapel was erected at the junction of Henry Street and Effingham Street in 1860. The old Zion chapel became a theatre, the Theatre Royal, until 1876 and was then the temperance hall until 1895. A new Baptist chapel was erected at the southern end of Westgate in 1837. In 1865 a breakaway faction from Masbrough Independent chapel founded the Rotherham

Congregational church on Doncaster Gate (now the Civic Theatre). The Independent College continued at Masbrough, reaching a low point in the 1840s when the trustees lost money on unwise railway investments. Its fortunes were restored by Dr F.J. Falding, who became tutor in 1851, paying off the debt and increasing the number of pupils from 5 in 1851 to 14 in 1856. After a boiler explosion on Christmas Eve 1860 caused much damage, it was decided to look for a new site. Land was purchased on Moorgate in 1872 and the new college, for 30 students, was opened in 1876. The new building was only in use for 12 years as the college merged with Airedale College, Bradford, in 1888. The Moorgate building and grounds, which had cost £26,000, were sold to the feoffees for £8,000, for use as new accommodation for the grammar school. By the 1870s the Unitarian chapel on Downs Row had become too small for its congregation. The foundation stone for a new chapel on Moorgate Street was laid on 1 May 1878 and the new chapel, known as the Church of Our Father, opened in February 1880. The old chapel was retained as a Sunday school.

The provision of poor relief was revolutionised by the Poor Law Amendment Act of 1834. This grouped parishes into poor law unions administered by elected boards of guardians. In the interests of economy (and lower poor rates) the poor were only given relief if they agreed to move into the new workhouses that sprang up in every union. Rotherham became the centre of a union stretching from Wath in the north to Aston in the south. Initially the board leased the parish workhouses at Rawmarsh, Laughton and Rotherham (in the Crofts). These were replaced in 1839 by a large new union workhouse erected on the hillside between Westgate and Moorgate, on a site purchased from the feoffees. There was accommodation for 200 inmates, soon increased to 300, with segregation of the sexes the rule, even for married couples. The workhouse infirmary was used as a hospital for the poorer classes but it was not until 1872 that the town had a proper hospital. In 1867 a meeting of inhabitants resolved to collect subscriptions to build a hospital, £500 being subscribed by Earl Fitzwilliam, £678 by the Earl of Effingham and £1,000 from Elizabeth Nightingale. The dispensary committee merged with the new hospital committee and Babbs Croft on Doncaster Gate was purchased as the hospital site. The foundation stone was laid on 19 January 1870 and the first patients were admitted to Doncaster Gate Hospital in May 1872.

In 1870 a public meeting resolved to petition the government to have Rotherham declared a borough. The petition was successful and on 29 August 1871 the royal charter of incorporation was received, covering the townships of Kimberworth and Rotherham. The borough council consisted of 18 elected councillors

The Victorian font in the parish church, with its cover in memory of the Rev. William Newton (d. 1879). (*Rotherham Central Library*)

St John's Church at Masbrough, one of several Victorian churches erected to serve the outlying areas of the town. (*Rotherham Central Library*)

The Primitive Methodist chapel, Wellgate, opened in 1851. It became the temperance hall after the new Primitive Methodist chapel was erected next door in 1893. (*Author*)

(three for each of six wards) who in turn elected six aldermen from among their own ranks, and a mayor. The first mayor was John Matthew Habershon, who had been chairman of the Local Board for some years. The Local Board had been planning a market hall for the town. The council took over these plans but it was not until 1879 that they were able to purchase and demolish the property around the market-place and erect an iron and glass market hall. This survived until January 1888 when it was destroyed by fire. The new brick market hall, opened on the same site in 1889, served the town until 1971. The cattle market remained important and by 1851 was selling around 3,000 sheep and 200 cattle each week. In 1865, however, an outbreak of the cattle disease rinderpest caused the magistrates to order the closure of the market. By the time it was reopened in 1867, a new Monday cattle market in Sheffield had stolen much of its trade.

Rotherham's first public park was the result of a campaign, headed by John Guest, to persuade the council to acquire Boston Castle and the land around it. Boston Park was opened on the appropriate date of 4 July 1876. In 1891 the council also purchased Clifton House and its grounds. The grounds became Clifton Park while the house became Rotherham's museum. In 1879 the council obtained powers to extend its boundaries, taking in part of Greasbrough, part of Brinsworth and the northern portion of Whiston. The original Local Board offices became inadequate and in 1895 the council acquired the adjoining temperance hall, savings bank and mechanics institute, remodelling the block into a new town hall and assembly rooms. Headquarters for the Rotherham Police Force,

Doncaster Gate Hospital opened in 1872. (*Rotherham Central Library*)

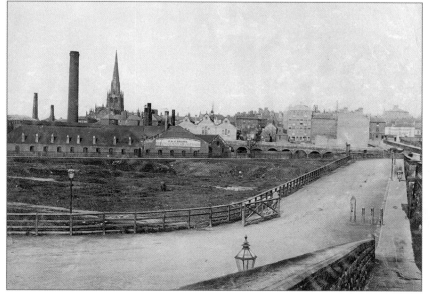

A panoramic view of the town centre taken from the Central station on Main Street. The first Market Hall (1879–88) can be seen in the centre with Rotherham Forge and Rolling Mill in the centre foreground. (*Rotherham Central Library*)

The mechanics institute at the corner of Howard Street and Effingham Street, *c.* 1885. To the left, on Howard Street, can be seen the temperance hall, the local board offices and the savings bank. (*Rotherham Central Library*)

The Crown Inn on High Street, photographed after the Election Riot of 21 July 1865, with some of the Hussars posed in the archway. (*Rotherham Central Library*)

founded in 1882, were erected on Frederick Street. The opening of the new public library and swimming baths on Main Street and the School of Art on Effingham Street marked Queen Victoria's Golden Jubilee in 1887.

Until the secret ballot was introduced parliamentary elections in Rotherham were often violent affairs. In 1865 a mob of Liberal supporters attacked the Crown Hotel, the Conservative headquarters, breaking most of the windows and knocking the Superintendent of Police off his horse. Order was restored by a troop of Hussars from Sheffield Barracks. The Crown was also damaged in an election riot in 1871, as was the Ship Hotel in 1880.

13

The Twentieth Century

Rotherham Borough Council entered the new century with a forward-looking adoption of new technology. The Rotherham Corporation Act of 1900 empowered the council to establish a modern electric tramways system radiating from the town centre. The three main lines were to run from a junction with the Sheffield Tramways at Tinsley, via Sheffield Road and the town centre to the new waterworks pumping station in Fitzwilliam Road; from Kimberworth Road, near Bradgate Lane, via Masbrough Street, Main Street, Westgate and Effingham Street to Rawmarsh boundary; and from Canklow to join the first-mentioned in Westgate. Most of the lines were to be single track with loops at intervals to allow trams to pass each other. The line to Tinsley provoked opposition from some councillors who felt that the council should not be making it easy for Rotherham residents to spend money in Sheffield.

At Masbrough the road passed under the Midland Railway with far too little headroom to allow trams to run. The corporation was empowered to enter into an agreement to lay tramlines over the new over-bridge planned by the railway company. Construction work on the tracks and poles began in July 1902 and 13 open top double-deck and three single-deck trams were ordered from Dick, Kerr of Preston. Following trial runs on 29 December 1902 and inspection of the route by the Board of Trade, the official opening of the system took place on 2 February 1903. A further 15 trams were ordered in March 1903 in anticipation of the opening of the Kimberworth route. On 7 April 1903 the mayoress opened the new Coronation Bridge at Masbrough, named in honour of the coronation of Edward VII. Initially the line at Tinsley was not connected to the Sheffield system, and it was only in

College Square and Effingham Street in the early years of the century, with Sheffield tram no. 174 waiting to depart. The Victorian courthouse stands at the right. (*Rotherham Central Library*)

One of the first batch of Rotherham trams at the Kimberworth terminus, *c.* 1905. The tramway's horse-drawn tower wagon, used for servicing the overhead cables, is passing the tram. (*Rotherham Central Library*)

1905 that the gap was bridged and through running became possible. New routes constructed under powers obtained in 1904 included an extension from the pumping station to the bottom of Whinney Hill, Dalton (opened 1906; extended to Thrybergh 1911) and a short line along Wellgate (1908–10) later extended along Broom Road to Herringthorpe Lane (authorised 1911). At the Rawmarsh boundary, the lines made a connection with the Mexborough and Swinton Traction Co. line via Rawmarsh and Swinton to Mexborough (authorised 1904, opened 1906). Corporation Street, authorised in 1900 to connect the market-place with Bridgegate and Frederick Street, was not built until 1913 when powers were obtained to construct a tramway from Westgate to Effingham Square. In 1912 Rotherham became the first municipality to operate trolley buses outside its own boundaries when a service was started from the tram terminus at Herringthorpe Lane to Maltby. The council purchased its first two motorbuses in 1913 to operate a service to Thorpe Hesley. A third was added in 1914 to operate services from Canklow to Treeton.

The power for both electric lighting and the tramways came from the new municipal power station erected on Rawmarsh Road in 1900. The supply was inaugurated on 23 May 1901 and originally came from four steam-driven generators capable of delivering 232 kilowatts. An additional 165-kilowatt set was added in 1902 in anticipation of the extra load expected from tramway use. Further extensions were made in 1903 and 1905; a 500-kilowatt steam turbine generator was added in 1908 followed by a 1,000-kilowatt set in 1918. Thereafter the power station was continually extended to keep abreast of demand.

At this period domestic refuse was collected in horse-drawn carts and tipped at Northfield. The refuse tip reached such a size that it was known popularly as Spion Kop (after the Boer War battle) or Mother Kush. The borough council decided to kill two birds with one stone by erecting a refuse destructor adjacent to the power station. Opened in 1909, the destructor burned 75 tons of domestic refuse a day to raise steam for the power station. This enabled the daily collections of refuse to be dealt with, but did but not allow any inroads to be made into Spion Kop.

In 1902 the town attained county borough status, giving the council the powers of a county council. The new county borough took over the local schools from the School Board in 1903 under the terms of the Balfour Education Act. It was the first Director of Education,

Spurley Hey (appointed in 1906), who pushed the council into making provision for older pupils by establishing two higher standard schools for boys and girls aged 11 to 14. The first of these opened in 1911 at South Grove, Moorgate, on the site of the former pupil teacher centre. The second was opened at Kimberworth in 1914. From 1906 the Grammar School was incorporated on the board of education's grants list and the borough council was empowered to nominate eight of the 15 governors. There was no equivalent school for girls until in 1903 the council purchased the private girls school run by Miss Law in her own house, Elmfield, Alma Road. A site was purchased on Middle Lane in 1908 and the new High School for Girls opened in 1910.

The construction of tramlines up the High Street only served to emphasise the narrowness of 'The Bottleneck' at the top of the street. In 1905 the council purchased the property on the north side of the High Street, between Church Street and the market-place. These buildings were demolished, as was the Shambles behind them, enabling the High Street to be widened. A new block of shops and offices, known as Imperial Buildings, was opened in 1908, to designs by local architect Joseph Platts. The new Talbot Lane Methodist

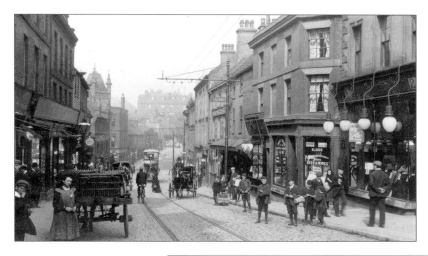

A view down the High Street, c. 1910. A tram has just passed down the street on its way to College Square and a private carriage is pulling away from J.H. Humphrey's pawnbroker's shop.

The Bottleneck at the top of the High Street, before the tram tracks were installed. The Shambles can be seen at the left. (*Rotherham Central Library*)

Rotherham Fire Brigade's horse-hauled steam fire engine, photographed at the Rawmarsh Road depot, *c.* 1910.

The Chapel on the Bridge and Rotherham Bridge, after the restoration of the chapel in 1924 but before the construction of Chantry Bridge in 1930. Note the wooden supports under the medieval arches. (*Rotherham Central Library*)

chapel in the Crofts opened in 1903. In November 1901 its predecessor had been destroyed by fire when an organ tuner dropped his candle into the organ. Although the volunteer fire brigade was on site within 15 minutes they were unable to save the building. It was this fire that decided the borough council to establish a permanent fire brigade. The new force, consisting of an inspector, horseman and 17 firemen, under the control of the chief constable, was based in a converted warehouse in Rawmarsh Road. Horse-drawn steam pumps were used until the first motor fire engine was purchased in 1914.

By the early years of the century there was increasing feeling that the continued use of the Chapel on the Bridge as a tobacconist's shop was a sacrilege. In 1901 a petition with almost 1,000 signatures was presented to the feoffees, calling for the chapel's restoration. Local architect J.E. Knight suggested that it might be restored for use as a museum and meeting place for the feoffees. Various obstacles were put in the way of the feoffees and it was not until 1913 that the tobacconist was bought out by Sir Charles Stoddart, former managing director of

Parkgate Iron and Steel Co. and mayor of Rotherham on four occasions (1886–7 and 1904–7). His death the same year thwarted his plans to restore the chapel as a place of worship. Anticipating the restoration, he bequeathed £500 to the vicar and churchwardens to be 'applied in or towards maintaining the services in the Chapel on the Bridge which I have repaired'. It was eventually agreed that the money should be handed over to the vicar and churchwardens provided that they repaired the chapel within 12 months of the end of the First World War. The structure was transferred to the Church Commissioners in 1918 but it was not until 1924 that the chapel was restored to designs by J.E. Knight and reconsecrated by the Bishop of Sheffield.

There was a choice of entertainment in the Edwardian era. In addition to numerous public houses, there were several theatres in the town centre. The Theatre Royal on Effingham Street had been opened in 1873, replacing the Alexandra Music Hall on Howard Street. This was in turn replaced by a new Theatre Royal, designed by Joseph Platts, at the junction of Howard Street and Nottingham Street in 1894. The largest theatre in the town was the Hippodrome on Henry Street, opened in 1908 with seats for 2,500. Its main rival was the Empire Theatre at the top of the High Street, opened in 1913 as a variety theatre and also equipped to show films. In the early years of the century the variety theatres came under increasing pressure from the new moving pictures. The first showing of films in Rotherham was Edison's Electric Bioscope, exhibited at the Statutes Fair in 1898. By 1900 travelling exhibitors were regularly putting on shows at the Clifton Hall or the Assembly Rooms. In 1902 Jasper Redfearn's exhibition of early sound films in the Assembly Rooms included footage of the return of the Rotherham Volunteers from the Boer War. The first permanent cinema was the Picture Palace (later Whitehall Cinema), opened in the Masonic Hall, High Street, in February 1911. The same year also saw the conversion of the Zion chapel on Howard Street into the Electric Pavilion (closed 1930). Patrons in Kimberworth and Masbrough had the choice of the Premier Picture Palace on Kimberworth Road (1912) and the Tivoli on Masbrough Street (1913). Finally in March 1914 the Cinema House, with its distinctive Moorish architecture, opened on Doncaster Gate.

The demolition of the Regent Theatre (formerly Theatre Royal) on Howard Street, in October 1957. The rear of the Hippodrome can be seen at the top left. (*Rotherham Central Library*)

No history of the town would be complete without mention of Rotherham United, the third football club in the town to attain Football League status. Rotherham Town were Midland League champions in 1891/2 and 1892/3. Elected to the Second Division of the Football League in 1893, they lasted until the 1895/6 season when financial problems forced them to drop out. The Thornhill United club changed its name to Rotherham County and moved to a new ground at Millmoor, Masbrough, in 1907. They won successive Midland League championships between 1911/12 and 1914/15, and were elected to the Second Division in 1919, the first post-war season. Financial problems led to the merger of Rotherham Town and Rotherham County in 1925 when the new club, Rotherham United, was admitted to the Second Division. They were founder members of the new Third Division (North) in 1922 and remained in that division until they were promoted, as champions, in 1950/1.

When the First World War broke out in August 1914, nobody can have envisaged the long list of local names that would appear on the town's war memorial eight years later. The men of Rotherham and district answered the call to arms, issued by the mayor, P. Bancroft Coward, with a will. The local Territorials, the Fifth Battalion, York and Lancaster Regiment, were mobilised and received a civic send-off when they went off to war from the Central station. In early September a recruiting meeting held in College Square attracted a crowd estimated at 10,000. The purpose of the meeting, to enlist 600 men to form a sixth battalion of the York and Lancs, was more than fulfilled, there being some 200 volunteers over towards a seventh battalion. By the end of the war the regiment had grown to 22 battalions and had seen active service on almost every front – France, Salonika, Egypt, Gallipoli, Italy, etc. News of casualties soon began to filter back from the front and, for the remainder of the war, each issue of the *Advertiser* carried photographs of men who were serving at the front, with sombre lists of the killed and injured and poignant pleas for information from the families of the missing.

In October the first Belgian civilian refugees arrived in Rotherham and were boarded at Thrybergh Hall as the guests of Rotherham Golf Club. Later batches of refugees were accommodated in Eastwood House. Twenty wounded Belgian soldiers were treated at Rotherham Hospital. Local industries turned to supporting the war effort, many of them

The announcement of the death of Edward VII and the accession of George V in 1910. Most of the volunteers of the 5th Battalion, York and Lancaster Regiment, drawn up in front of the Court House, would be marching off to war four years later. (*Rotherham Central Library*)

The main business of Owen and Dyson was the forging of railway wheels and axles. During the First World War they turned over to manufacturing shells, as seen here. (*Rotherham Central Library*)

converting to produce shell casings and munitions, while the demand for coal kept the local pits busy. In April 1915, in response to an appeal to raise additional brigades of artillery, the council recruiting committee decided to raise a howitzer brigade of four batteries and 633 men. The 164 (Rotherham) Howitzer Brigade, Royal Field Artillery, was soon up to complement and its initial training was held in Clifton Park. In June 1915 the mayor reviewed a grand military parade in the park with 4,000 troops and a military band. This was followed by a recruiting meeting in the tram sheds on Rawmarsh Road, addressed by the bellicose Horatio Bottomley, editor of *John Bull*. The Howitzer Brigade left Rotherham in July for further training elsewhere in Yorkshire and on Salisbury Plain. By January 1916 they were at the front in France. In September a heavy battery of the Royal Garrison Artillery was raised in the town within three weeks. George V made an informal visit to Steel, Peech and Tozer in October 1915, part of a campaign to raise the morale of the workforce. The same year saw a number of anti-German disturbances in the town, with the shops of German butchers such as Limbach and Schonhut bearing the brunt of the mob's rage. Oakwood Hall was converted into a military hospital in 1916. VAD nurses ministered to casualties and convalescing soldiers in hospital blue uniforms became a common sight in the town.

The demand for steel was such that Steel, Peech and Tozer were asked to extend their plant at Templeborough, over the site of the Roman fort. Following the excavation of the fort site, the Templeborough Melting Shop, with 14 open-hearth furnaces was erected. Its ¼-mile long roof and 14 chimneys were local landmarks until the 1960s. In September 1917 the steelworks at Parkgate was the target for a Zeppelin raid but only minor damage was caused. A 200 lb unexploded Zeppelin bomb was excavated at Templeborough in 1961. When peace finally came on 11 November 1918 there was general rejoicing and dancing in the streets of the town. On a sadder note, the Armistice coincided with a major outbreak of influenza that caused many deaths in the area. The medical officer of health's report for 1918 recorded 294 deaths from epidemic influenza.

A captured German gun joined the two Victorian naval guns behind Clifton Park Museum and a British tank was installed on the base that formerly supported the bandstand in Clifton Park. The tank only lasted until 1927 when the council voted for it to be broken

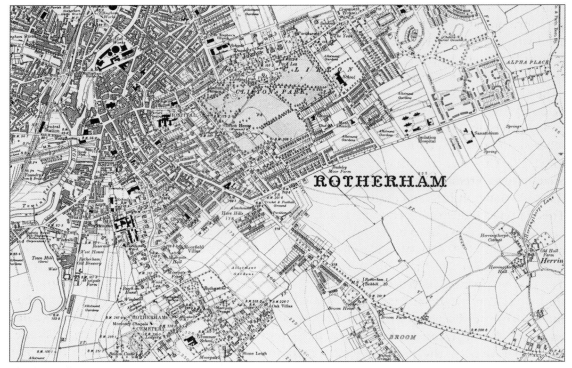

Rotherham in 1924 showing the start of the council housing development at East Dene (off Far Lane). (*Ordnance Survey sheet 289SE*)

up with any proceeds from the sale of the scrap going to military charities. A new bandstand was erected on the site in 1928. The other guns lasted until 1937 when the *Advertiser* was of the opinion that they would be better used as scrap in the local steel furnaces. In 1919 work began on compiling the long list of Rotherham's war casualties. Lt. Col. J.E. Knight was commissioned to design the war memorial in Clifton Park, unveiled on 26 November 1922 in the presence of the Bishop of Sheffield and Lt. Gen. Sir Ivor Maxse. Bronze plaques recorded the names of 1,304 Rotherham men who had given their lives for their country. Another war memorial can be seen in the south aisle of the parish church.

During the war the Government had calculated that there would be a projected shortfall of 1,000,000 houses when the war ended. Councils were required to take steps to build their share of the necessary housing. A housing committee had been formed in 1913 and in 1916–17 the council had purchased land for housing at East Dene and at Hilltop, Kimberworth. The Council estimated in 1919 that 3,000 houses would be needed, of which 2,090 were to meet unsatisfied need, overcrowding and population growth. The scheme first drawn up in 1916 had to be expanded and a further 109 acres at East Dene was purchased from the Earl of Effingham. A scheme was drawn up to build 1,000 three-bedroom houses, the first being ready for occupation in May 1920. By the end of 1925 1,016 new houses had been built in the borough (192 by private enterprise) and there was a waiting list of 1,500. Further houses were built on the Herringthorpe estate from 1924 and a number of two-bedroom houses, for the 'lower working class', were erected at Hartington Road, Meadow Bank Road and Canklow Road. The availability of council houses enabled the borough council to start clearing many of the slum houses in the town. In 1933 and 1934 eleven clearance orders were issued, covering 258 houses and the insanitary courts of houses that lined streets such as Westgate and Wellgate began to be swept away. By 1939 1,196 unfit houses had been demolished and their occupants rehoused, and the council had erected a total of 4,943 houses at 32.98 houses per 1,000 population, twice the national average.

Steel, Peech and Tozer had ended the war with a fine new steel plant and was confident of doing well in post-war conditions, expecting to step in and take the markets that had previously been filled by the German steel industry. The partners felt that an alliance with other steelmakers would improve their position and United Steel Companies Ltd was formed in 1918. This was an alliance of Steel, Peech and Tozer, Samuel Fox and Co. Ltd of Stocksbridge, Frodingham Iron and Steel Co. Ltd and Appleby Iron Co. Ltd of Scunthorpe (Lin), Workington Iron and Steel Co. Ltd of Workington (Wes) and Rother Vale Collieries Ltd. The expected industrial expansion would have increased the demand for electricity so the borough council began to build a new, larger power station on Rawmarsh Road with a total capacity of 55,000 kilowatts. It came into operation in 1920 but was not officially opened until 1923 when the Prince of Wales performed the ceremony during a visit to Rotherham. The post-war period, however, was an era of commercial instability with world trade thrown into confusion by the collapse of many currencies. Rotherham suffered like most other manufacturing districts in the post-war slump. High unemployment and pressure from employers for wage cuts led to political unrest and Communist gatherings in College Square, and clashes with the police became common. One of many measures to alleviate unemployment was the board of guardians' scheme to offer employment dismantling Spion Kop, which finally disappeared from the skyline. In April 1921, during a three-month coal strike, 8,800 men were registered with Rotherham Employment Exchange, rising to 10,000 in May. In June a body of unemployed men, carrying a banner inscribed 'death is better than semi-starvation', marched to the workhouse to interview the guardians. When the coal commission called for further wage cuts in 1926, the miners struck again. The dispute escalated until the TUC called a General Strike from 3 May, resulting in the closure of all the collieries, steelworks, public transport and other works in the area. Although the General Strike only lasted nine days, the miners stayed out until the autumn, causing much distress. In July over 400 miners from the Wath area marched to Rotherham Workhouse and demanded admission, claiming to be destitute. When they then marched to the police station, there were violent clashes with the mounted police. The long coal strike and its consequent distress almost bankrupted the Rotherham Board of Guardians, who had to suspend poor relief until the Government bailed them out. The rule of the guardians came to an end in 1929 when their powers, within the Borough of Rotherham, were transferred to the council. Although the workhouse was renamed the Public Assistance Institution, it lost none of its terror for the poorer inhabitants of the town.

In 1930 the number of unemployed stood at 15,000, 15.6 per cent of the male workforce and 11.1 per cent of females, and the town was declared a depressed area. A number of the national hunger marches of the early 1930s passed through Rotherham. In October 1931 a reduction in benefits provoked a march of 4,000 men from the fairground site in Main Street to the town hall, where the ruling Labour Party refused to receive a deputation. A baton charge by the police broke up the crowd. An advance party from Burnley (Lan), arriving in October 1932, were entertained to tea by the local branch of the National Union of Unemployed Workers. In the evening they addressed a meeting in Corporation Street, attacking the passivity of the

The newly built Herringthorpe Valley Road looking south, with newly erected council houses in the Shelley Drive area in the background. (*Rotherham Central Libaray*)

Private housing development on East Bawtry Road (nos 400–50), erected in advance of the road widening, 1937. (*Rotherham Central Library*)

audience and the local Labour Party. Later in 1932 marchers from Scotland were accommodated at the Institution and were then entertained to breakfast at the True Briton in Westgate, headquarters of the local Communist Party. Participants in the last big hunger march, in 1936, were put up at the assembly rooms and entertained at the cinema and the swimming baths. The Labour Party had first taken control of the borough council in 1928 when Ald. Sam Hall served as mayor. The parliamentary seat was first won for Labour in 1923 by F.W. Lindley who defeated the sitting Independent member, Maj. F.W. Kelly.

In 1924–5 the Rotherham Regional Town Planning Committee employed W.R. Davidge to produce a regional planning scheme. His proposals included improved road and rail services, the designation of industrial and residential areas and open spaces and a number of new roads to stimulate industry. Among his road schemes was an industrial development road on the north side of the Don from Masbrough through Parkgate to Swinton and Wath, another on the south side from Aldwarke Lane through Thrybergh Park to Denaby, a 100 ft wide road up Herringthorpe Valley and a road from Whiston to Catcliffe. Most of these were never built. Herringthorpe Valley Road was first contemplated in 1920 as a scheme for the employment of ex-servicemen. In the event, however, the council decided to build Meadow Bank Road. Herringthorpe Valley Road was finally constructed as a joint venture with West Riding County Council, 75 per cent of the cost being paid by the Ministry of Transport. The Earl of Harwood opened the new road in 1933. Within the town centre the medieval bridge had begun to show signs of wear and the arches had to be supported with wooden braces. Rather than demolish the ancient structure, the council built a new, reinforced concrete bridge a few yards upstream. Herbert Morrison, Minister of Transport, opened Chantry Bridge on 28 April 1930. The old bridge was reduced to its medieval dimensions and remained in use as a footbridge. The year 1930 also saw the purchase of the Herringthorpe estate, with other land on Badsley Moor Lane and Broom Road. Most of the land was earmarked for housing but a large area was set aside as Herringthorpe playing fields. Another road to be upgraded was Castle Sike Lane, connecting Whiston crossroads with Broom Lane and the Brecks. This became a dual carriageway road, renamed East Bawtry Road, and opened in 1937. By this time suburban development had already begun to stretch along the line of the new road that fell just within the borough as a result of an expansion of Rotherham's boundaries in 1936. In that year the urban district of Greasbrough with parts of Whiston, Brinsworth and Dalton were absorbed within the borough. In 1931 the population of the county borough had been 69,689 within an area of 5,895 acres. In 1936 the acreage increased to 9,258 and the population to 74,600.

The 1920s and 1930s saw many changes in the town centre. The cattle market in the Crofts was chosen as the site of a new West Riding court house. A new cattle market, opened in 1926, was built on the west side of Corporation Street. Construction of the court house (now the town hall) involved the demolition of the island of buildings between the Crofts and Talbot Lane, including the Cross Keys and Black Swan. A new Cross Keys was erected on Moorgate Street. When the library on Main Street was badly damaged by fire in 1925, it moved into a wooden hut on Corporation Street until 1931 when the new public library on Howard Street opened. The swimming pools beneath the old library continued in use until 1968. They were supplemented by new, larger swimming baths in Sheffield Road, opened in 1936. With the development of bus and trolleybus services, the council decided that a proper terminus was needed. The property between College Street and the Churchyard was cleared and laid out as All Saints' Square, opened in 1933. To enable vehicles to travel into the new square it was necessary to widen Bridgegate by demolishing all the property on the west side (including the timber-framed Turf Tavern) and rebuilding further back. The College of Technology and Art on Howard Street (1931) gave a new home to the art, technical and commercial instruction that had been conducted in the School of Art on Effingham Street. New schools constructed between the wars included primary schools in Badsley Moor Lane (1925) and Coleridge Road (1940) and a new Central School in Cranworth Road (Spurley Hey, 1931). The gasworks on Frederick Street ceased to produce gas from coal in 1928 as plentiful supplies of gas were available from local steelworks. By 1938 the town was taking 1,820 million cu. ft of gas from the steelworks and the old gasholders and purification plant were in need of renewal. It was decided to move to a new gasworks at Car House where a 2,000,000 cu. ft waterless gasholder was erected in 1938. The new fire station on Erskine Road was opened in 1939, just in time for the beginning of the Second World War.

All Rotherham's theatres were converted into cinemas between the wars – the Empire in 1921 and the Hippodrome in 1932. The Theatre Royal on Howard Street had been converted for cinema and variety in 1915. In 1930 it was converted into a sound cinema, under the

Bomb damage at the corner of Harrison Street and Rutland Street in the Holmes area after the air raid of 29 August 1940. (*Rotherham Central Library*)

name the Regent, but was converted back to a variety theatre in 1935. A new luxury cinema, the Regal, was built on Corporation Street in 1934. It contained an elaborate Conacher cinema organ, used for radio broadcasts by the resident organist, Dando.

Air raid precautions had been introduced in 1938 and the population knew what to do when the air raid sirens sounded after Neville Chamberlain's announcement of the outbreak of war. Some Rotherham children were evacuated to Kiveton Park but returned home when air raids failed to materialise. A large proportion of the civilian inhabitants were soon heavily involved in the Home Front, whether as members of the Home Guard, as air raid wardens or fire watchers or as members of the Auxiliary Fire Service. A number of anti-aircraft gun sites were established in the area to protect the industries in the Don Valley and Clifton Park was chosen as a barrage balloon site. Part of Herringthorpe playing fields was ploughed up to increase food production.

Luckily Rotherham suffered little from the attentions of the Luftwaffe during the war. There were only two serious air raids on the town, on the nights of 19 and 29 August 1940, when the steelworks at Templeborough seems to have been the target. Two people were killed during the first raid when four bombs damaged the British Oxygen factory in Armer Street. The second raid caused extensive damage to houses in the Holmes area and one bomb hit the offices and stables of the Midland Iron Works. Windows were damaged over a wide area of the town. Some incendiaries fell on Rotherham during the Sheffield blitz of December 1940 but did little damage. In 1972 a 1,000 lb unexploded bomb was discovered in the goods yard at Masbrough.

The York and Lancaster Regiment was again in the thick of the fighting, its battalions serving in France, Norway, Palestine, Crete, North Africa, Tunisia, Italy, Greece, India and Burma. The local Territorial battalion, the Fifth, had been re-raised in 1920 and converted into an anti-aircraft regiment in 1936. As the 67th (York and Lancaster) Heavy Anti-Aircraft Regiment, RA, it served in Egypt, India and Burma.

The townsfolk responded eagerly to the fund raising during the various 'Warship Weeks' and similar campaigns. In August 1940, during the Battle of Britain, the *Advertiser* launched an appeal to raise £4,000 to purchase a Spitfire or Hurricane. Spitfire VB, no.

R7298, first flew in April 1941, bearing the name 'Rotherham District'. The aircraft had a distinguished career with various RAF and USAF squadrons before it crashed in Shropshire during a training flight in November 1944, killing its Polish pilot. In 1942 the town raised some £700,000 during 'Warship Week' which enabled the town to adopt HMS *Rotherham*, an 'R' Class destroyer, launched in March 1942. Assigned to 11th Destroyer Flotilla, based at Trincomalee, Ceylon, the destroyer was to earn fame as the ship that accepted the surrender of the Japanese in Singapore on 5 September 1945. Members of her Royal Navy crew have retained close contacts with the town.

As in the First World War many local factories were turned over to war production. Guest and Chrimes and John Baker and Bessemer converted their factories to produce armaments. Robert Jenkins were among numerous factories around the country to produce sections of the war-winning Bailey Bridge, designed by Rotherham-born Donald Bailey. With so many men in the forces, women were recruited to work in many of the factories including Steel, Peech and Tozer and Parkgate Iron and Steel. As people could not get away for holidays, the council

A reminder that the designer of the war-winning Bailey Bridge was born in Rotherham, this example acts as a footbridge over the Don at Eastwood. It is shown during repairs carried out in 1992. (*Rotherham Central Library*)

One of the roundabouts in Clifton Park, part of the council's 'Holidays at Home' celebrations during the war, *c.* 1943. (*Rotherham Central Library*)

arranged 'Holidays at Home' during the summer with roundabouts and entertainments in Clifton Park, concerts and sports. A lone German plane, which dropped four bombs in the Clifton area in August 1942, was thought to have mistaken the 'Holidays at Home' tents for a military camp.

The post-war era saw increasing changes in the town. As soon as the end of the war was in sight, the housing committee began to plan the post-war programme and started building roads and sewers on the East Herringthorpe site in February 1945. An initial batch of prefabricated houses was erected in Mowbray Gardens in March 1945 with conventional house building advancing in parallel. House building continued in the 1950s and 1960s with new estates arising in Broom Valley, Kimberworth Park and Wingfield. The council was not seduced by the fashion for building upwards and only erected one modest tower block, Beeversleigh on Clifton Lane (1970–1). Not all the council's developments were successes. The St Ann's Road flats, erected in 1966–7 using the 'Bison' system, soon ran into trouble with decaying concrete and faulty heating. Despite having won a commendation from the Ministry of Housing in 1969, the flats were demolished in 1987 and replaced with low-density sheltered housing. Oakhill Flats at Eastwood, a complex of 607 flats and maisonettes, was erected in 1970–1 and received a 'highly commended' in the 1974 Department of the Environment Housing Awards. By the late 1990s the complex no longer met current housing needs, and most of it was demolished and replaced with lower density housing.

Local industries, particularly the steel and coal industries, have faced an uncertain future since 1945. Some old-established companies have disappeared completely. J.J. Habershon and Sons took over their neighbours, Peter Stubs, but were themselves taken over by GKN and closed in 1981. Yates and Haywood were taken over by William Heaton Holdings Ltd in 1967 and closed in 1971. The frontage of their factory still exists, minus the portion that was demolished to make way for Centenary Way. The hammers at Sheffield Forge and Rolling Mills dominated the town centre until 1981. The Forge Island site was cleared to make way for Hillard's supermarket (now Tesco). Guest and Chrimes survived on Don Street until late 1999 when their new French owners moved production to Derbyshire. The steel industry remained a major employer but suffered its share of ups and downs in the post-war era. Nationalised by the Labour Government in 1951, Steel, Peech and Tozer were denationalised in 1953. Brinsworth Strip Mill was erected on the south side of Sheffield Road in 1955–8. The distinctive chimneys of the Templeborough Melting Shop disappeared in 1960–3 when the open-hearth furnaces were replaced with six electric arc furnaces. The company was nationalised once more in 1967, becoming part of British Steel. More recent years have seen yet another privatisation, as Rotherham Engineering Steels, reabsortion into British Steel and transfer to the Anglo-Dutch group Corus. Steelmaking at Templeborough ceased in 1993 and the buildings are currently being converted into MAGNA, an iron and steel museum.

Increased need for secondary education as a result of the 1944 Education Act led to the building of new schools at Old Hall, Kimberworth (1959), St Bernard's Catholic school (1961) and Wingfield (1965). Selective boys' and girls' technical high schools were opened at Oakwood, Moorgate, in 1952–3, becoming general secondary schools in 1960. Only the Grammar School and the High School retained selection until 1967 when comprehensive education was introduced. The Grammar School became Thomas Rotherham Sixth Form College while the High School became Clifton Comprehensive. With the loss of resident population in the town centre, South Grove School closed in 1987. Spurley Hey School closed in 1991, the buildings being taken over as an upper school for Clifton Comprehensive.

A view south from St Ann's Road in 1967 with Effingham Square in the background. Work had started on clearing the houses on Effingham Street, Norfolk Street and Tusmore Street to make way for the civic buildings and other council offices. The new bus station was already in use, top right. (*Rotherham Central Library*)

Between the wars the tram routes were gradually replaced by motorbus and trolleybus services. By 1949 the only tram route remaining was the line to Tinsley and Sheffield. When the bridge at Tinsley needed rebuilding, the through line was cut and Sheffield City Council never reinstated the tracks over the new bridge. There was little point in keeping the line open on the Rotherham side and the last tram ran on 13 November 1949. There was considerable investment in trolleybuses in the 1950s but by the early 1960s trolleybus operation was becoming increasingly uneconomic and in 1963 a policy of gradual abandonment was agreed. The last trolleybus ran in October 1965. All Saints Square ceased to be the main transport interchange in 1971 when the bus services moved to the new bus station on the site of the former gas works. The Square became a pedestrian precinct with fountains and flowerbeds.

Under the terms of the National Health Service Act 1946 the responsibility for hospitals in the borough passed to the Sheffield Regional Hospital Board in 1948. The general hospitals at Doncaster Gate, and the Municipal General Hospital, Moorgate, with the infectious diseases hospitals at Badsley Moor Lane and Kimberworth and the Oakwood Hall Sanatorium were administered by the Rotherham and Mexborough Hospital Management Committee. This arrangement lasted until the health service reorganisation of 1974 when the Rotherham hospitals passed to Rotherham Area Health Authority, part of the Trent Regional Health Authority. Following the opening of the first phase of the new District General Hospital in the grounds of Oakwood Hall, Moorgate, in 1978, Moorgate Hospital (the former workhouse infirmary) was closed and demolished.

The spread of television in the 1950s and 1960s and, latterly, the popularity of out-of-town multi-screen cinemas, eventually led to the closure of all Rotherham's cinemas. The Regent Theatre closed in 1957, followed by the Hippodrome (1959), Tivoli (1959), Whitehall (1960), Premier (1961) and Cinema House (1964). The Empire, later renamed the Essoldo and later still the Classic, closed as the Cannon in 1990 and was turned into a complex of bars. The Regal (later the Odeon and the Scala) closed in 1983 and is now a bingo hall. The town did, however, gain a theatre in 1960. When the Doncaster Gate Congregational church closed, it was taken over by the borough council and converted into the Civic Theatre. Other churches and chapels to be closed since the war include the Ebenezer chapel and the Church of Our Father (both now mosques), St John's, Masbrough (demolished), Masbrough Independent chapel (carpet and furniture warehouse) and the Primitive Methodist chapel, Wellgate (Masonic Hall). Since 1945 Rotherham United has had a chequered career in the Football League, moving upwards and downwards between the old Second and Fourth Divisions, despite having had a selection of high profile managers, including Tommy Docherty and Emlyn Hughes. The club were losing finalists (to Aston Villa) in the first League Cup Final in 1961 and tasted Wembley glory when they won the Auto Windscreens Shield Final in 1996. In the 1980s and 1990s Rotherham Rugby Club began a climb through the local and national leagues that saw them challenging for promotion to the first division at the end of the 1999/2000 season.

The construction of the M1 motorway, opened to Tinsley in 1968, had a profound effect on the long distance traffic through the town centre. At the same period the inner ring road, Centenary Way, bypassed the town centre, resulting in the demolition of much property in Masbrough. The first phase, from St Ann's Road to Greasbrough Road, opened in June 1969. Phases two and three, extending the road to Bow Bridge, were completed in 1975. Two further phases, to Canklow and to Rotherway (1991 and 1995), completed the dual carriageway through to the M1 at Junction 33. With most of the traffic routed away from the town centre, the council was able to embark on a scheme of pedestrianisation. By the late 1990s the High Street, College Road, Effingham Street, Howard Street and Bridgegate had all been pedestrianised. The decision to move the market to a new site between Howard Street and Wharncliffe Hill in 1971 moved the centre of gravity of the town centre northwards and the High Street began to suffer as a result. The construction of new shops on the New Zealand site, between Howard Street and Bridgegate (the Cascades Centre), in 1984 only

The first phase of Centenary Way, photographed in 1970 when traffic was still light. The flyover connects the new road with Effingham Square. (*Rotherham Central Library*)

A view across the northern part of the town from the roof of Rotherham College on Howard Street, 1973. The power station and its cooling towers are prominent. The gasholder at Car House can be glimpsed between the two cooling towers. The roof of the Centenary Market is at bottom right and the multi-storey car park, above the bus station, is in the centre. (*Rotherham Central Library*)

All Saints Square in 1999, shortly before work began to clear the fountains and flower beds and completely relay the square to a new design. (*Author*)

served to reinforce the trend. The construction of the shopping centre at Meadowhall, just over the border in Sheffield, was also to have a profound effect on the town centre shops.

The early 1970s saw a growing complex of council offices erected in the area bounded by Nottingham Street, St Ann's Road and Effingham Street – Crinoline House, Civic Building, Norfolk House and the Central Library and Arts Centre, opened in 1976 to replace the old Howard Street library. The borough council celebrated its centenary in 1971 but three years later it disappeared as a result of the 1972 Local Government Act. In 1974 Rotherham became the centre of the Metropolitan Borough of Rotherham, comprising the county borough with the urban districts of Maltby, Rawmarsh, Swinton and Wath and the rural districts of Rotherham and Kiveton Park. The area controlled by the council increased from 9,167 acres and 84,801 people in 1971 to 69,869 acres and a population of 243,131 in 1974. By 1991 the population had risen to 247,776. The year 1974 also saw the transfer of the borough's bus services to the South Yorkshire Passenger Transport Executive. Rotherham's police force had been amalgamated with that of Sheffield in 1967, with the combined force becoming part of South Yorkshire Police in 1974. The fire brigade became part of South Yorkshire Fire Service. The old town hall on Howard Street soon became too small for the enlarged council, and in 1988 the council moved to temporary accommodation in the transport offices on Frederick Street and the town hall was converted into a shopping arcade. Following the opening of the new court house, at the rear of the police headquarters on Main Street, in 1994, the court house in the Crofts became redundant. It was acquired by the council and converted into a new town hall, opened in 1995.

On the last day of 1999 a time traveller from AD 1 would have looked in disbelief at the changes that had taken place in the area over 2,000 years. Successive waves of invaders, Romans, Angles, Normans, etc., have all left their mark on the area, as have the ravages of the industrial revolution. Rotherham's growth and development has not been a story of continual improvement and prosperity and recent decades have seen the decline of the two staple industries upon which the town's industrial prosperity had been based. In 1996 unemployment in the borough stood at 13 per cent. The last decade has, however, seen a slow recovery with derelict industrial sites being regenerated, unemployment falling to 7 per cent and the town centre fighting back against the threat of out-of-town shopping complexes. The modern inhabitant of Rotherham can look back on a proud heritage and a promising future.

Select Bibliography

Guest, John, *Historic notices of Rotherham* (Robert White, Worksop, 1879). No history of Rotherham would be possible without Guest's monumental (708 page) work that has preserved the text of many documents that have since been lost. Unfortunately the index is less than user-friendly and obscures many of the gems in the text.

A lifetime in steel (Rotherham Libraries, 1987). An illustrated history of the iron and steel industry in the town.

Armitage, Harold, *Rotherham's forerunners* (West Yorkshire Printing Company Ltd, 1953). A history of the area up to the departure of the Romans.

Bennett, Rev. Henry Leigh, *Archbishop Rotherham* (J.W. Ruddock, Lincoln, 1901)

Blazeby, Rev. William, *Rotherham: the Old Meeting House and its ministers* (H. Garnett, Rotherham, 1906) A history of the Unitarian Church in the town.

Crowder, Freda, and Dorothy Greene, *Rotherham* (SR Publishers Ltd, 1971). Published to coincide with the borough council's centenary, this volume combines Freda Crowder's short history of the town with Dorothy Greene's histories of the parish church and the Chapel on the Bridge.

Guest, John, *Relics and records of men and manufactures at or in the neighbourhood of Rotherham* (A. Gilling, Rotherham, 1865, reprinted by Rotherham Libraries, 1980).

Hall, Charles C., *Rotherham and district transport*, 3 vols (Rotherwood Press, Rotherham, 1996–9). A definitive history of public transport in Rotherham, from stage coaches to motorbuses.

Hunter. Rev. Joseph, *South Yorkshire* (2 vols 1828–31, reprinted).

John, A.H., *Minutes relating to Messrs. Samuel Walker & Co., Rotherham* (Council for the Preservation of Business Archives, 1951).

Jones, Mel (ed.), *Aspects of Rotherham*, 3 vols (Wharncliffe Publishing, Barnsley, 1995, 1996, 1998). The *Aspects* series comprises a series of articles on aspects of the Rotherham area by experts in the field.

Jones, Mel, *Rotherham's woodland heritage* (Rotherwood Press, Rotherham, 1995). A study of the biology and industrial archaeology of the historic woodland around Rotherham.

May, Thomas, *The Roman forts of Templeborough near Rotherham* (Rotherham Borough Council, 1922). An exhaustive account of the finds discovered during May's excavations during 1916–17.

Munford, Anthony P., *Rotherham; a pictorial history* (Phillimore and Co., Chichester, 1994). A short history of the town, illustrated with over 150 photographs.

Simpson, Grace, 'Roman Manchester and Templeborough: the forts and their dates reviewed', in Christopher and Sonia Hawkes (eds.), *Greeks, Celts and Romans; studies in venture and resistance* (J.M. Dent and Sons Ltd, London, 1973). A re-evaluation of the dating of the fort based on the pottery found by May.

Smith, Howard, *A history of Rotherham's roads and transport* (Rotherham Libraries, 1992). The story of Rotherham's roads from prehistoric times to the twentieth century.

Thornes, V.M., *The health of Rotherham: a short history of health services in the Rotherham area* (Rotherham Libraries, 1980).

Index